Toffees, Fudges, Chocolates and Sweets

Toffees, Fudges, Chocolates and Sweets

MARY NORWAK

PELHAM BOOKS

First published in Great Britain by
PELHAM BOOKS LTD
52 Bedford Square
London WC1B 3EF
1977

ISBN 0 7207 0956 3

Printed in Great Britain by
Northumberland Press Ltd
Gateshead

Contents

Acknowledgements

My particular thanks are due to Davis Gelatine Ltd and C H Dempster & Co Ltd (Kake Brand) for their help with technical advice and recipe testing.

Introduction

Does anything remind us so much of childhood as the memories of the sweets we used to eat? Toffee apples and sugar mice, barley sugar sticks and treacle toffee, coconut ice and acid drops, giant pear drops and Edinburgh rock, winter boilings and sherbet, gradually gave way to the more adult tastes of fondant, marzipan and truffles, but all take their place in our reminiscences. We used to buy them in tiny sweet shops from tall glass jars, sometimes wrapped in triangular 'pokes', or from stalls at bazaars and fêtes, parting with precious halfpennies and pennies.

Today's standardisation has meant the end of many old favourites. Most of our confectionery now is neatly packaged in standard sizes, frequently chocolate-based, and few childhood favourites linger on. Liquorice boot-laces and sherbert dabs are still available and sugar mice appear at Christmas time, enterprising greengrocers sometimes produce toffee apples and one or two travelling sweet stalls still visit fairgrounds with a variety of home-made goodies. The average confectioner can offer little but prewrapped bars and a few boiled sweets and toffees, so if we crave the old favourites, we must make our own.

Sweetmaking is not difficult, and equipment and ingredients are usually on hand. Many of us had our first experience of cooking as children, making sweets when we couldn't be outdoors.

Peppermint creams are the traditional starting point for budding cooks, working up to truffles. When the stove can be used safely, fudge, coconut ice and toffee quickly follow. All the recipes in this book are easy and delicious, but those which are suitable for children to make without supervision are indicated*.

1 Equipment and Ingredients

It is not necessary to buy extra or expensive equipment for home sweetmaking. It is perfectly possible to use everyday kitchen tools, but if more ambitious work is planned, one or two special items may be useful.

EVERYDAY EQUIPMENT

Wooden Spoons and Spatulas. These should be used for sweet-making, and it is a good idea to keep them separately from those normally used in the kitchen so that they remain clean. Make sure they have long handles so the hand remains well away from any boiling mixtures being stirred. A spatula is particularly useful for working fondant and beating fudge.

Saucepans. These should be large, strong, deep and thick-based, preferably with slightly rounded bottoms. Brass, copper, stainless steel and aluminium are all good, but enamel will not stand up to the high temperatures necessary. Cheap thin pans will burn quickly; shallow pans allow moisture to evaporate quickly and often when a sugar thermometer is used, the thermometer bulb will not be properly covered.

Palette Knife. A very flexible stainless-steel blade is useful for lifting and shaping sweets.

Marble Slab. This is often recommended as many sweets need to be poured out on to a cold surface for shaping. An enamelled surface can be used instead, but many plastic surfaces will not stand a temperature above 280°F/140°C so laminated table tops are not always suitable.

Tins. Straight-sided oblong or square tins should be used. A square 7 in. or 8 in. tin is useful for most recipes, and a Swiss-roll tin is also a useful size.

Strong Scissors. These are needed for cutting some types of toffees.

Pastry Brush. This is useful for brushing egg white on sweets for sticking layers together.

Sugar-boiling Thermometer. This is not absolutely necessary, but does take the guesswork out of sweetmaking (see Chapter 3: Sugar Boiling Temperatures) and is in any case a useful piece of kitchen equipment. Choose an easy-to-read, well-graduated thermometer preferably with a sliding clip to fit over the pan side. To prepare a new thermometer, put it in cold water, bring to the boil and leave it in the water to cool.

Waxed and Greaseproof Paper. Buy in sheets or save from cereal packets.

Meat Skewers, Lolly Sticks and Cocktail Sticks. These can be stored for use with toffee apples, etc.

SPECIAL EQUIPMENT

The items listed below are for more ambitious sweetmaking and can be bought as needed. They are obtainable from:

T Errington & Son		United Yeast Co Ltd
Southsea Works	*and*	Crown House
Rodney Road		Morden, Surrey
Milton, Portsmouth		

Rubber Fondant Mats. These can be used for fondant, jelly and chocolate shapes.

Starch Tray and Plaster Moulds. Used for shaping fondants.

Cream Rings. These metal circles can also be used for moulding creams.

Dipping Forks. Small forks for lifting sweets from coating fondant or chocolate and for marking patterns.

Candy Bars. These bars are oiled and placed on an oiled slab so that they enclose an area into which to pour mixtures. They can be adjusted to give the exact size and thickness required of such items as toffee.

Caramel Marker. A set of metal squares can be used to press on the surface of caramels, toffees and candies before they are set to mark them into neat squares.

INGREDIENTS

Like equipment, most of the ingredients for sweetmaking are normally found in the kitchen and special purchases are rarely necessary. However one or two points should be noted:

Butter. Fresh, unsalted butter is best for sweetmaking. Small quantities of margarine can be used, but large quantities will not be readily absorbed.

Sugars. Granulated, caster, icing, soft brown and demerara sugars are all useful. Cube sugar is sometimes recommended.

Honey and Golden Syrup. These give a delicious flavour to many sweets, but should be used in the correct proportions (i.e. 4 oz to 1 ½ lb sugar). Their use means that sweets do not crystallise so readily.

Glucose. This helps to prevent crystallisation, but sweets made with glucose soften more quickly. It is therefore most useful in fondant type sweets. It can be used in powder form but liquid glucose is used professionally, keeps almost indefinitely and may be bought at large chemists.

Cream of Tartar. This also helps to prevent crystallisation, but does not have the softening effect of glucose.

Cornflour. This is used in some jelly sweets, and for coating sweets and storage puposes.

Rice Paper. This is needed for finishing nougat.

Gum Arabic. Crystals can be bought at the chemist and are used for crystallisation of flowers and for varnishing marzipan.

Milk. Evaporated and sweetened condensed milk are often used in sweetmaking and are worth keeping in stock. The recipes specify the type to be used.

Colourings. Pure vegetable colourings should be used. Green, yellow and red are the most useful basic colours and can be mixed for a variety of effects.

Decorations. Chocolate vermicelli, grated chocolate, cocoa powder, drinking chocolate powder, crystallised flower petals, silver balls, angelica and glacé cherries are easily obtainable from bakers, confectioners and grocers.

Flavourings. Natural flavourings, e.g. lemon juice, should be used wherever possible, but some fruit juices are not concentrated enough and can make mixtures too moist, so essences have to be used instead. Oils are stronger and have a better flavour than essences and should be used where obtainable (this is particularly true of peppermint and lemon). Rum, brandy and liqueurs give excellent flavour and richness to sweets and can be bought in miniature sizes.

2 *General Sweetmaking Rules*

1. See that all equipment is scrupulously clean and ready for use.
2. Collect all the ingredients beforehand and weigh them out carefully.
3. Dissolve sugar carefully in water or liquid at a low temperature before boiling and do not stir.
4. If crystals start to form around the sides of the pan, brush them down with a clean pastry brush dipped in cold water.
5. Do not stir the mixture unless the recipe specifies this as sugar mixtures 'grain' quickly and this is not required for all types of sweets. In general, mixtures which contain fat, milk and treacle need gentle stirring occasionally to prevent burning. Fat in the mixture will also make the brushing down of crystals unnecessary.

6. Some recipes suggest that a cover should be put on the pan for the first few minutes of boiling. This helps to reduce the formation of crystals, but the lid must be removed when the temperature rises above 212°F/100°C.

7. Check temperatures carefully by thermometer or more homely methods (see Chapter 3: Sugar Boiling Temperatures). At high temperatures, the heat of the pan will cause the temperature of mixtures to rise still further, so it is best to remove the pan from the heat at about 5°F/3°C before the correct temperature. If the base of the pan is quickly put into cold water, it will keep the temperature steady, but it must not be left too long or the mixture will solidify too quickly.

8. Flavour and colour sweets carefully. They are best added from the tip of a skewer or a teaspoon. Hard, bright colours and over-strong flavours are unattractive.

9. Cut sweets into neat squares or circles, and even sizes. Avoid fancy shapes.

10. To prevent stickiness, wrap toffees in paper as soon as they are cold. Fudges should not be wrapped. Store sweets in polythene boxes or tins, but do not try to keep them too long or they will dry out.

3 Sugar Boiling Temperatures

A thermometer is recommended for successful sweetmaking, but for most sweets it is possible to assess temperature by using practical, more homely methods.

USING A THERMOMETER

Put the thermometer into a bowl of warm water while the sugar is being dissolved. When the sugar is ready, wipe the thermometer and put it into the mixture, ensuring that the bulb is covered. Read the temperature at eye level. When the correct temperature is reached, put the thermometer at once into a bowl of warm water. Wash carefully so that no mixture is left sticking to the bulb, and dry carefully.

TEMPERATURES

Sweetmaking temperatures have identifying names which correspond to the type of sweet being made. These names, together with homely tests for temperature assessment, are given in the list below. When using the homely tests, put some very cold water into a small cup and have it ready for testing constantly—temperatures rise quickly and the mixture can go past the correct stage very rapidly. Throughout the recipes, temperatures are accompanied by their identifying names for easy reference, but while the identifying names indicate the homely tests, exact temperatures should be adhered to where possible.

SMOOTH—220°F/105°C—for crystallising
The mixture looks syrupy. Dip the fingers into cold water and very quickly into the syrup. The thumb will slide smoothly over the fingers, but the sugar will cling to the fingers.

SOFT BALL—237°F/114°C—for fudge and fondants
Pour a little syrup into very cold water. It will form a soft ball when rolled in the fingers.

HARD BALL—247°F/119°C—for caramels, marshmallows and nougat
Drop into cold water. The mixture will form a firm ball which holds its shape, but is still plastic.

SOFT CRACK—280°F/140°C—for toffee
A drop in cold water will separate into threads which are hard but not brittle.

HARD CRACK—310°F/154°C—for hard toffee and rock
A drop in cold water separates into threads which are hard and brittle. A thin piece snaps easily. Once this temperature has been reached the toffee will be brittle and will not stick to the teeth.

CARAMEL—340°/171°C—for praline

The syrup becomes golden brown or 'caramel' colour. The colour becomes darker as the temperature rises, but above 350°F/175°C the mixture will taste burnt.

4 Toffees, Butterscotch and Caramels

Care must be taken not to burn the hot syrup used in toffee-making, and an asbestos mat is advised if gas is used. Put the mixture into a large saucepan so that it cannot boil over, and brush round the inside of the pan with olive oil, just above the surface of the syrup, which will prevent the mixture bubbling too high in the pan. Heat the mixture gently until the syrup has dissolved before boiling. Do not stir the mixture unless the recipe indicates that this should be done. If a thermometer is used, move it in the pan from time to time so that toffee does not stick to the bulb and give an inaccurate reading.

Keep the heat low under the pan when the temperature reaches

260°F/125°C (i.e. between hard ball and soft crack) and take the pan off the heat when the mixture reaches a temperature about 5°F/3°C below the figure required, because the pan will hold heat and the mixture may be over-boiled. If a thermometer is not used keep a cup of ice-cold water handy and test the mixture frequently. Add fruit and/or nuts which have been slightly warmed.

Pour the mixture into a greased tin or a marble slab as soon as it is ready. Oiled candy bars, which can be pressed together to give the thickness of toffee required, can be used on a slab. The toffee should be marked into squares with a caramel marker or knife before it is completely set. Toffee should be wiped free of oil or grease with kitchen paper, and wrapped in waxed paper for storage.

Pulled toffee makes attractive sweets. The toffee can be formed into a sausage shape when cool enough to handle, then pulled, folded, twisted and pulled with oiled hands until the required effect is obtained. The toffee should look satiny and silvery. The best method of pulling toffee is to use a large hook firmly fixed at a convenient height. Be sure the hook is clean and oiled. Oil the hands and throw the toffee over the hook. Catch it and pull it, repeating the process until the right colour is obtained.

Pulled toffee can be formed into cushions by shaping the toffee into a 1 in. diameter roll, and cutting off inch-long pieces with oiled scissors, twisting them slightly as you do so. Pulled and un-pulled toffee may be twisted together and formed into cushions or sticks.

PLAIN TOFFEE
    3 oz butter
    5 oz granulated sugar
    1 large can sweetened condensed milk
    1 tablespoon golden syrup
    Few drops vanilla essence

Melt the butter and sugar together, and add the milk and syrup. Boil slowly for 20 minutes, stirring all the time. Boil to 310°F/ 154°C (hard crack). Before removing from the heat, flavour with a little vanilla essence. Pour into a well-greased tin and when cool, mark into squares.

GINGER TOFFEE

    2 lb brown sugar
    1 large teaspoon ground ginger
    1 oz butter
    1/4 pint white vinegar

Put the sugar and ginger into a saucepan and mix well, then add the butter and vinegar. Heat very gently until the sugar dissolves, then bring to the boil. Boil steadily until the temperature reaches 310°F/154°C (hard crack). Pour into a greased tin and when cold, break into pieces.

BLACK JACK TOFFEE

    12 oz butter
    8 oz black treacle
    1 lb Barbados sugar
    1 large can sweetened condensed milk
    2 teaspoons vanilla essence

Melt the butter and add the treacle, sugar and milk. Bring slowly to the boil and stir for about 35 minutes to 310°F/154°C (hard crack). Stir in the vanilla essence and pour into a greased tin. When half set, mark into squares. Break into squares when set.

SCOTCH TOFFEE

    1 lb granulated sugar
    1/4 pint water
    2 oz butter
    1 small can sweetened condensed milk
    1 teaspoon vanilla essence

Dissolve the sugar carefully in the water, add the butter and con-densed milk and heat until dissolved. Boil to 280°F/140°C (soft crack), stirring gently. Add the vanilla essence and pour into a greased tin. When cool, mark into squares, and cut when cold.

CREAMY TOFFEE
    1 lb cube sugar
    good ¼ pint water
    1 good tablespoon powdered glucose
    3 oz butter
    1 small can sweetened condensed milk
    1 teaspoon orange essence

Place sugar and water in a large saucepan and heat gently until the sugar has dissolved. Strain and add the glucose, and boil with-out stirring to 237°F/114°C (soft ball). Stir in the butter gently, a small piece at a time, until each piece is absorbed. Stir in the condensed milk. Continue to boil steadily to 280°F/140°C (soft crack). For best results, check heat carefully after 260°F/125°C with a sugar thermometer. Pour into a greased tin. Mark when half cold and cut when set.

TREACLE TOFFEE (1)
    1 lb brown sugar
    8 oz black treacle
    2 oz butter
    2 tablespoons water
    1 tablespoon malt vinegar

Put all the ingredients into a large pan. Dissolve the sugar very slowly and then boil for about 20 minutes to 280°F/140°C (soft crack). Pour into a greased tin and mark into squares when beginning to set.

TREACLE TOFFEE (2)

    4 oz butter
    8 oz granulated sugar
    3 tablespoons black treacle
    2 tablespoons malt vinegar

Melt the butter in a large thick saucepan. Add all the other ingredients and stir until the sugar has dissolved. Bring to the boil and boil quickly for about 10 minutes to 247°F/119°C (hard ball). Pour into a greased tin and mark into pieces while still warm. Break when cold.

PULLED TREACLE TOFFEE (TOM TROT)

    1 lb granulated sugar
    1 lb black treacle
    1 oz butter
    1 dessertspoon malt vinegar

Put the sugar, treacle and butter into a thick saucepan and heat very gently until the sugar has melted. Stir until boiling and then cook to 247°F/119°C (hard ball). Take from the heat and stir in the vinegar. Pour into a tin until cool enough to handle. Oil the hands and a strong hook and put the piece of toffee over this. Pull it rapidly with both hands until it is too hard to work any longer, twist it and then cut it in pieces with oiled scissors. This is a Yorkshire toffee eaten round the bonfire on Guy Fawkes' Night.

SCOTS CREAMY CANDY

    2 lb icing sugar
    ½ pint water
    Large pinch cream of tartar
    Few drops of flavouring (peppermint or ginger)

Melt the butter in a thick saucepan. Add the sugars, chocolate, syrup and milk. Bring to the boil, then continue to boil for about 15 minutes, stirring all the time, to 280°F/140°C (soft crack). Add the essence and pour the mixture into a greased tin. Mark into squares when cool and break up when cold.

HELENSBURGH TOFFEE

>   2 lb granulated sugar
>   4 oz butter
>   4 fl oz water
>   1 large tin sweetened condensed milk
>   Few drops vanilla essence
>   4 oz walnut kernels

Put the sugar, butter and water into a thick saucepan. Stir over a gentle heat until the butter and sugar have melted. Add the condensed milk and stir continuously over a gentle heat for 45 minutes. Take off the heat, add the essence and stir for one minute. Pour into a greased tin and mark into squares when cool. Put a walnut half on each square. Break into pieces when cold.

BUTTERSCOTCH

>   6 oz butter
>   1 lb soft brown sugar
>   8 oz golden syrup
>   1 tablespoon water
>   Pinch of cream of tartar
>   ½ teaspoon vanilla essence
>   ½ teaspoon lemon essence

Melt the butter in a heavy saucepan and add the sugar, syrup and water. Melt slowly over a low heat. Bring to the boil, add the cream of tartar and boil to 280°F/140°C (soft crack). Add the essences and pour into a greased tin. Mark into squares when the toffee has cooled a little and break into pieces when cold.

RUSSIAN TOFFEE

1 lb granulated sugar
4 oz butter
2 tablespoons water
4 fl oz single cream
½ teaspoon vanilla essence

Put the sugar, butter and water into a heavy saucepan and stir over a low heat until boiling. Take off the heat and stir in the cream. Boil again until the mixture is thick and creamy at 247°F/119°C (hard ball). Take off the heat and stir in the essence. When the mixture stops boiling, pour into a greased tin. Mark into squares when the toffee is cool; break into pieces when cold.

EVERTON TOFFEE

8 fl oz water
1 lb demerara sugar
8 oz butter
2 teaspoons lemon juice

Heat the water and sugar gently until the sugar has dissolved. Boil to 310°F/154°C (hard crack). Add the butter and lemon juice and beat until melted. Pour into a greased tin and mark when cool.

CHOCOLATE ALMOND CRUNCH

1 tablespoon hot water
1 tablespoon powdered coffee
8 oz caster sugar
6 oz butter
6 oz split almonds, toasted
4 oz plain chocolate

Put the water, coffee, caster sugar and butter in a saucepan and heat gently, stirring all the time, until the sugar is dissolved. Boil until the mixture reaches 280°F/140°C (soft crack). Remove from the heat. Add 4 oz of the split almonds. Pour into a greased baking tray and spread evenly. Chop the remaining 2 oz of almonds coarsely. When the toffee is cool, break the chocolate into small pieces and melt in a basin over a pan of hot water. Spread the melted chocolate over the toffee, sprinkle with the chopped almonds and leave to harden. Break into pieces when cold.

PEPPERMINT TOFFEE

> 1 lb golden syrup
> 2 oz butter
> Few drops oil of peppermint

Cook the syrup and butter very gently together, stirring occasionally, to 280°F/140°C (soft crack). Add the oil of peppermint and pour into a greased tin. Break into pieces when cold.

GINGER ALMOND TOFFEE

> 1 lb soft brown sugar
> 8 oz butter
> 2 tablespoons golden syrup
> ½ teaspoon ground ginger
> Juice of 1 lemon
> 2 oz blanched, split almonds

Put the sugar and butter into a saucepan and heat gently until melted. Add the syrup, ginger and lemon juice. Boil hard to 280°F/140°C (soft crack). Remove from the heat and stir in the split almonds. Pour into a greased tin and break into pieces when cold.

ALMOND TREACLE TOFFEE

    2 oz almonds
    1 lb soft brown sugar
    ¼ pint water
    2 oz butter
    1 tablespoon golden syrup
    1 tablespoon black treacle
    Pinch of cream of tartar
    1 teaspoon lemon juice

Blanch the almonds, shred and brown them lightly under the grill, then place in the bottom of a greased tin. Put the sugar into a large saucepan with the water and stir over a low heat until all the sugar is dissolved. Add the butter, syrup, treacle and cream of tartar. Boil rapidly, stirring occasionally, to 310°F/154°C (hard crack). Add the lemon juice without stirring and pour at once over the almonds in the tin. When beginning to set, mark into squares. When cold, break into squares and wrap in waxed paper.

BROWN HAZELNUT TOFFEE

    4 oz hazelnuts
    8 oz soft brown sugar
    2 oz butter
    2 tablespoons golden syrup
    1 ½ tablespoons water
    2 teaspoons malt vinegar

Put the nuts into boiling water, drain them and rub off the skins. Dry them well and put on to a baking sheet and brown at 350°F/175°C (Gas Mark 4) for 15 minutes. Put the sugar, butter, syrup, water and vinegar into a heavy saucepan. Stir over a low heat until the sugar has dissolved, then boil quickly for 12 minutes. Stir in the nuts and pour into a greased tin. Break into pieces when cold.

ALMOND HARDBAKE

1 lb cube sugar
1 teaspoon cream of tartar
½ pint water
4 oz blanched almonds

Put the sugar, cream of tartar and water into a heavy saucepan. Heat gently until the sugar has dissolved and then boil until it begins to turn golden, i.e. to about 310°F/154°C (hard crack). Stir in the almonds and pour into a greased tin. Break into pieces when cold.

NUT TOFFEE

1 lb granulated sugar
¼ pint water
1 tablespoon malt vinegar
1 oz butter
6 oz nuts, toasted and chopped
Pinch of salt
1 teaspoon vanilla essence

Put all the ingredients except the nuts into a saucepan, and stir until dissolved. Bring to the boil and cook steadily to 310°F/154°C (hard crack). Add the chopped nuts to the toffee. Pour into a greased tin and when cold, break into pieces.

WALNUT TOFFEE

1 lb granulated sugar
3 oz butter
Scant 4 fl oz water
¼ teaspoon cream of tartar
3 oz walnut kernels

Brush a tin with oil and arrange the walnut kernels flat side up in rows. Put the sugar, butter and water into a thick saucepan and bring to the boil. Stir in the cream of tartar and boil without stirring to 280°F/140°C (soft crack). Pour into the tin and mark into squares just before the toffee sets.

COUNTRY WALNUT TOFFEE

    4 oz butter
    8 oz soft brown sugar
    8 oz golden syrup
    4 oz walnut kernels

Melt the butter in a thick saucepan. Stir in the sugar and syrup. Boil and stir to 280°F/140°C (soft crack). Chop the walnuts roughly. Take the toffee from the heat and stir in the nuts. Pour into a greased tin and mark into squares when nearly set. Break when cold.

PULLED TOFFEE

    1 lb granulated sugar
    1/4 pint water
    1/4 level teaspoon cream of tartar
    1 tablespoon water
    1 good tablespoon golden syrup or 2 oz powdered glucose
    Flavouring, as required
    Colouring, as required

Place the sugar and 1/4 pint of water in a pan and heat gently until the sugar has dissolved. Strain. Dissolve the cream of tartar in a tablespoonful of water and mix with the golden syrup or glucose. Add this to the pan and boil to 247°F/119°C (hard ball). Reduce heat and boil gently to 310°F/154°C (hard crack). (This higher boil gives a crisper sweet.) Remove from heat and place bottom of pan in cold water for 5 seconds. Pour the syrup on to an oiled slab or tin. Pour flavouring and colouring over the centre. Fold edges to middle with an oiled palette knife. Continue till toffee can be handled, then pull till stiff and satiny. Quickly cut into cushions or humbug shapes with oiled scissors.

HUMBUGS: For striped humbugs divide syrup into two portions. Add colour to one and pull slightly less than the plain batch. Then pull the two together once or twice and cut up as before.

FLAVOURINGS: Oils are preferable as they are more concentrated. Use ¼-½ teaspoonful oil of peppermint, lemon, etc., to 1 lb sugar or stir 2 teaspoonsful flavouring essence gently into the syrup before pouring on the slab.

NOTE: Pulled sweets must be wrapped when cold in generous squares of cellophane or waxed paper and stored in airtight containers.

BARLEY SUGAR

    1 lb granulated sugar
    ¼ pint water
    ¼ level teaspoon cream of tartar
    1 tablespoon water
    1 tablespoon golden syrup
    2 teaspoons lemon essence

Place the sugar and water in a pan, and heat gently until the sugar has dissolved. Strain and mix in the cream of tartar dissolved in 1 tablespoon water, and the golden syrup. Boil to 247°F/ 119°C (hard ball) then lower the heat and boil gently to 310°F/ 154°C (hard crack). Remove from the heat and immediately place the bottom of the pan in cold water for 5 seconds to cool the contents. Very gently stir in lemon essence to flavour. Pour on to an oiled slab or tin. When firm enough cut in strips, twist and place on a cool part of oiled slab to get cold. Wrap in waxed paper or cellophane. Store in tins or screw-top jars.

CINDER TOFFEE

8 oz granulated sugar
1 tablespoon golden syrup
¼ teaspoon cream of tartar
2½ fl oz water
¼ teaspoon bicarbonate of soda
1 teaspoon warm water

Put the sugar, syrup, cream of tartar and water into a heavy saucepan and heat gently until the sugar has dissolved. Boil to 310°F/154°C (hard crack). Dissolve the bicarbonate of soda in the warm water and pour it into the toffee, which will froth up. Stir and pour into a greased tin. Break into pieces when cold.

PUFF CANDY

2 lb demerara sugar
½ pint cold water
2 level teaspoons bicarbonate of soda

Put the sugar and water in a large, heavy saucepan. Heat gently until the sugar has dissolved to 310°F/154°C (hard crack). Remove from the heat and add the bicarbonate of soda. Stir well and pour at once into a greased roasting tin. When half cold, cut into small oblongs or squares, or leave until cold and crack with a hammer.

HONEYCOMB TOFFEE

6 oz granulated sugar
2 tablespoons honey
2 tablespoons golden syrup
2 tablespoons water
1½ teaspoons bicarbonate of soda

Place the sugar, honey, syrup and water in a large saucepan and dissolve over low heat, stirring occasionally. When the sugar has dissolved, bring to the boil, then reduce the heat and cook for 12-15 minutes to 310°F/154°C (hard crack). Remove from the heat and stir in the bicarbonate of soda. The toffee will then froth and form a honeycomb. Pour into a greased tin and when cold, break into pieces.

NOTE: Be sure to use a thick saucepan or the syrup may overheat and burn.

COFFEE CARAMEL (1)

>   1 lb granulated sugar
>   1 lb golden syrup
>   ½ pint evaporated milk
>   1 tablespoon coffee essence

Put the sugar, syrup and milk into a heavy saucepan and heat gently until the sugar has dissolved. Boil to 247°F/119°C (hard ball). Stir in the essence, but do not heat. Pour into an oiled tin. Mark into squares when cool. When cold, break into squares and wrap in waxed paper.

COFFEE CARAMEL (2)

>   3 oz granulated sugar
>   3 tablespoons golden syrup
>   1 small can evaporated milk made up to ½ pint with water
>   2 level teaspoons powdered coffee dissolved in ¼ pint boiling water
>   1 small can sweetened condensed milk
>   2 teaspoons vanilla essence

Put the sugar, syrup, evaporated milk and coffee into a saucepan, and heat until the sugar is dissolved. Bring to the boil, stirring all the time, then simmer gently for 15 minutes stirring occasionally. Add the condensed milk gradually and heat, stirring to 247°F/119°C (hard ball). Remove from the heat, stir in the vanilla essence, and pour into a greased tin. When cool, mark into squares and cut when cold. Wrap in waxed paper.

CHOCOLATE CARAMEL
       8 oz granulated sugar
       3 oz butter
       8 oz plain chocolate
       2½ fl oz single cream

Put the sugar and butter into a thick saucepan and dissolve over gentle heat, stirring well. Grate the chocolate and add it to the sugar, together with the cream. Bring to the boil and continue boiling and stirring to 280°F/140°C (soft crack). Pour into a greased tin. Mark into squares while still warm, and cut up when cold.

WALNUT MOLASSES
       2 oz walnuts
       1 lb soft brown sugar
       ¼ pint water
       Pinch of cream of tartar
       1 oz butter

Before making the sweet, toast the walnuts in the oven for 10 minutes, and then chop them roughly. Put the sugar, water and cream of tartar in a heavy saucepan and heat gently until the sugar has melted. Heat to 280°F/140°C (soft crack) and add the butter. Pour on to a slab in a long shape, and sprinkle with the walnuts. Fold over with a wooden spoon or spatula. When slightly cool, roll with the hands and pull out until about the thickness of a thin walking stick. Cut quickly in pieces with oiled scissors and wrap in waxed paper. This sweet quickly becomes sticky if left unwrapped.

TOFFEE GRAPES
        8 oz white grapes
        6 oz demerara sugar
        8 oz golden syrup
        2 oz butter

Divide the grapes into sprigs of two or three and hang them from a piece of string between two nails. Put the sugar, syrup and butter into a large, thick pan and stir until the mixture boils. Boil for 15 minutes to 280°F/140°C (soft crack). Cool the mixture slightly, then dip in one sprig of grapes at a time and hang it on the string. Handle the grapes quickly and do not leave them to stand in the toffee or they will cook.

BLACK BALL
        1 lb black treacle
        2 lb granulated sugar
        3 oz butter
        1 teaspoon ground ginger
        1 teaspoon lemon juice

Put all the ingredients into a heavy saucepan and heat gently until the sugar dissolves. Boil hard to 280°F/140°C (soft crack). Pour into a greased tin and mark into squares as it cools.

SWEDISH STRIPED CANDY
        1 lb granulated sugar
        8 fl oz water
        1 tablespoon powdered glucose
        2 tablespoons malt vinegar
        3 drops oil of peppermint
        Few drops of red colouring

Mix the sugar, water, glucose and vinegar in a thick saucepan and
leave to stand until dissolved. Bring quickly to the boil and cook
to 280°F/140°C (soft crack). Take off the heat and leave to cool
for 5 minutes. Pour three-quarters of the mixture on to an oiled
baking sheet and flavour with the peppermint oil, folding the
edges of the toffee in with a spatula. When the mixture is cold
enough to handle, oil the hands and fold, stretch and fold the
toffee continuously until thick and pale. Pull into 1 in. long
strips and put on to an oiled baking sheet. Colour the remaining
mixture with the red colouring and pour in two strips, one on
either side of the white toffee. Twist the strips together and cut
at once into shapes with oiled scissors.

AMERICAN CANDY

    1 lb cube sugar
    4 oz powdered glucose
    ¼ pint water
    3 oz butter
    Few drops of vanilla essence

Put the sugar, glucose and water into a heavy saucepan and heat
gently until the sugar has dissolved. Boil to 280°F/140°C (soft
crack). Add the butter in small pieces and boil to 310°F/154°C
(hard crack). Pour the mixture on to a greased slab and add a
few drops of essence. Fold over and over with a wooden spoon
or spatula and when sufficiently cool, work well with the hands
and pull into a long roll until it begins to stiffen. Cut in pieces with
oiled scissors and wrap in waxed paper.

5 Nougat

Nougat will store for about two weeks, but tends to become soft and sticky. It should be made with rice paper on top and bottom, then wrapped in waxed paper and stored in an airtight tin to keep it firm and compact. For making nougat, a hand-held electric mixer is useful, as it can be worked with one hand while syrup is poured on to egg whites with the other. Nougat is best made in a deep, rectangular tin. If a piece of cardboard is cut to the size of the tin, it can be placed on top and easily weighted to give a compact sweet. When lining a tin with rice paper, it is helpful to moisten the sides of the tin with water, as this makes the rice paper adhere better.

SIMPLE NOUGAT

8 oz blanched almonds
4 oz honey
4 oz icing sugar
2 egg whites

Neatly line a tin with waxed paper. Chop the almonds roughly. Put the honey, sugar and egg whites into a heavy pan and heat gently until the mixture is thick and white, to 247°F/119°C (hard ball). Put in the almonds, and then turn the nougat on to a slab dredged with icing sugar. Form the mixture into a ball and press it into the prepared tin. Cover with more wax paper and put under pressure by weighing down with another tin of similar size containing heavy weights. The nougat will be more professional if a piece of rice paper is put on top of the waxed paper under the nougat. The sweet should then be topped with rice paper and then waxed paper before pressing down with weights.

HONEY NOUGAT

6 oz honey
8 oz granulated sugar
Pinch of salt
4 fl oz water
2 egg whites
Few drops of vanilla essence
4 oz chopped nuts

Stir the honey, sugar, salt and water together over a low heat until the sugar has dissolved and the mixture begins to boil. Boil without stirring to 247°F/119°C (hard ball). Beat the egg whites very stiffly. Pour the hot syrup on to the egg whites, beating all the time. Add the flavouring and nuts. Line a tin with waxed paper and then rice paper. Pour in the nougat and top with rice paper. Mark into squares as the mixture cools.

ALMOND NOUGAT

    4 oz blanched almonds
    2 oz angelica
    1 lb granulated sugar
    8 oz powdered glucose
    ¼ pint water
    2 egg whites

Brown the almonds in the oven and chop them roughly. Chop the angelica. Put the sugar, glucose and water into a heavy saucepan and heat gently until the sugar dissolves. Boil to 280°F/140°C (soft crack). Beat the egg whites until stiff, then beat in the hot syrup gradually. When the mixture becomes thick, stir in the almonds and angelica and pour into a tin lined with rice paper. Cover with rice paper and press down with a heavy weight. Leave for 12 hours before cutting.

FRUIT NOUGAT

    1 lb icing sugar
    4 oz clear honey
    4 egg whites
    3 oz almonds
    1 oz pistachio nuts
    2 oz glacé cherries

Sieve the sugar and put it into a bowl standing in a saucepan of boiling water. Add the honey and the egg whites and whisk until the mixture is thick and white, which will take about 30 minutes. Cut the almonds and pistachios into shreds and chop the cherries. Grease a small deep tin and put a piece of rice paper in the bottom. Take the nougat off the heat, add the nuts and cherries and pour into the tin. Press well down and cover with more rice paper. Put a weight on top. Do not cut until cold.

MONTELIMAR NOUGAT

>12 oz granulated sugar
>¼ pint water
>3 oz powdered glucose
>3 oz honey
>2 small egg whites
>1 oz angelica
>2 oz glacé cherries
>5 oz shredded almonds
>½ teaspoon vanilla essence

For best results, use of a sugar-boiling thermometer is recommended.

Dissolve the sugar in the water over gentle heat. Add the glucose and boil to 266°F/130°C (midway between hard ball and soft crack). Put the honey in a bowl over hot water and heat gently until melted. Whisk the egg whites stiffly and stir into the honey. Pour on to the hot syrup, whisking well all the time. Add the sliced angelica and cherries, and the almonds and essence. Pour into a tin lined with waxed paper topped with rice paper. Put a piece of rice paper and waxed paper on top of the nougat and press under a weight until cold.

CHOCOLATE NOUGAT

>1 lb granulated sugar
>¼ pint water
>4 oz powdered glucose
>2 oz butter
>2 egg whites
>2 oz plain chocolate
>4 oz blanched almonds, chopped

Put the sugar and water into a heavy saucepan and heat gently until the sugar has dissolved. Add the glucose and butter and boil to 280°F/140°C (soft crack). Beat the egg whites to a stiff froth.

Pour on to the hot syrup gradually, beating all the time. Put the mixture in a bowl over boiling water and continue beating until the mixture forms a stiff ball when tested in cold water. Break the chocolate into small pieces, melt it in a bowl over a pan of hot water and stir it into the mixture, together with the chopped almonds. Put into a tin lined with rice paper. Top with more rice paper and cool under weights.

RASPBERRY NOYAU

> 14 oz granulated sugar
> $\frac{1}{4}$ pint water
> 3 oz liquid glucose
> 2 oz sieved raspberry jam
> Few drops of pink colouring
> 3 oz blanched almonds

Heat the sugar and water gently until the sugar has dissolved. Add the glucose and boil to 247°F/119°C (soft ball). Take off the heat and put into a bowl rinsed in cold water. Leave until luke-warm then add the jam and a little colouring. Stir until the mixture is soft and creamy then work in the almonds. Put into a tin lined with rice paper, and spread it to about $\frac{1}{2}$ in. thick. Cover with more rice paper and put on a heavy weight. The sweet may be varied by using warm melted honey instead of jam

6 Fudges, Tablets and Candy

Basically, fudge is made by boiling together sugar, butter, and milk or cream, although there are a few unboiled fudges which rely on melted chocolate and icing sugar to firm them. If the fudge contains milk, it must be stirred during cooking as it tends to burn. Stirring must be gentle or the mixture will begin to grain before it has been cooked thoroughly and the fudge will be rough and coarse. When cooking is completed, the fudge should be beaten until thick and creamy, without its glossy look. If you like short, crumbly fudge, go on beating until the mixture begins to set round the edge of the pan. Fudge can be melted down if it starts to harden too quickly. Fudge is easier to beat if the pan is tilted slightly so that the syrup is deep. The wooden spoon should be drawn through the entire depth of the mixture and not kept to the surface. Cream of tartar and glucose should not be added to fudge as they prevent successful 'graining' which produces the correct texture. Basic fudge can be flavoured with chocolate, coffee, a variety of essences or liqueurs, nuts, dried and glacé fruit.

'Tablet' is a Scots version of fudge, traditionally flavoured with cinnamon, coconut, figs, ginger, orange, lemon, peppermint, vanilla or walnuts. Candy is also included in this section, as the ingredients are similar to those for fudge but boiled to a higher temperature to give a firmer texture.

UNCOOKED CHOCOLATE FUDGE (1)*

4 oz plain chocolate, roughly broken
2 oz butter
4 tablespoons evaporated milk
Grated rind of 1 orange
1 lb icing sugar

Melt the chocolate and butter in a bowl over a pan of hot water. Add the evaporated milk and grated orange rind and mix well. Work in the sifted icing sugar until the mixture is quite stiff. Pour into a greased tin. Cut into squares when set.

UNCOOKED CHOCOLATE FUDGE (2)*

8 oz plain chocolate
4 oz butter
1 egg
1 lb icing sugar
2 fl oz sweetened condensed milk
4 oz chopped mixed nuts

Break the chocolate into small pieces and melt it with the butter in a double saucepan or in a bowl over hot water. Beat the egg lightly and add it to the sugar and milk. Stir well and add the melted chocolate and butter. Beat well and stir in the nuts. Put into a greased tin and chill in the refrigerator. Cut into squares when cold. This fudge stores well in a freezer and is useful to make ahead of school holidays.

UNCOOKED CHOCOLATE FUDGE (3)*
    2 oz plain chocolate
    1 oz butter
    1 small tin sweetened condensed milk
    8 oz soft brown sugar
    8 oz icing sugar

Break the chocolate into small pieces, melt it in a bowl over hot water, beat in the butter, then stir in the milk. Add the soft brown sugar and stir in. Sieve the icing sugar into the mixture and knead well until soft and creamy looking. Press into a lightly greased tin. Leave to set and cut into 1 in. squares.

UNCOOKED CHOCOLATE CREAM FUDGE*
    4 oz plain chocolate, roughly broken
    2 oz butter
    3 tablespoons single cream
    1 teaspoon vanilla essence
    1 lb icing sugar

Put the chocolate and butter into a saucepan over hot water. Melt slowly, stirring a little to blend together. Take the chocolate from the heat and stir in the cream and essence. Gradually work in the icing sugar and mix well. Put into a buttered greased tin and leave until cool, firm and set. As a variation, add 4 teaspoons coffee powder to the melted chocolate.

CRUMB FUDGE*
    6 oz biscuit, cake or bread crumbs
    2 tablespoons golden syrup
    2 oz butter
    2 oz granulated sugar
    2 oz cocoa
    Few drops vanilla essence

Rub the crumbs finely and crisp them lightly in the oven. Warm the syrup, butter, sugar and cocoa until they melt and blend. Stir the essence and crumbs into the syrup mixture and mix thoroughly. Press into a greased tin and mark into squares. Leave for 24 hours before cutting.

SHERRY FUDGE*

 2 tablespoons seedless raisins
 Sherry
 4 oz plain chocolate, broken
 2 oz butter
 4 tablespoons evaporated milk
 12 oz sieved icing sugar

Soak the raisins in sherry overnight. Place the chocolate and butter in a mixing basin over hot, not boiling, water. Stir until melted and smooth. Remove from heat, stir in the evaporated milk and drained, soaked raisins. Gradually stir in the sieved icing sugar until the fudge is smooth and thick. Turn into a buttered, waxed-paper-lined tin. Leave to cool. When set, remove from tin, peel away paper and cut into squares.

PLAIN FUDGE

 1 lb granulated sugar
 2 oz butter
 ¼ pint evaporated milk
 ¼ pint water
 ½ teaspoon vanilla essence

Put the sugar, butter, evaporated milk and water into a heavy saucepan and heat gently until the butter has melted and the sugar has dissolved. Bring to the boil and heat to 237°F/114°C (soft ball), stirring often. Take off the heat, add the essence and beat until smooth and creamy. Pour into a greased tin and mark into squares when nearly set.

MILK FUDGE

½ pint milk
1¾ lb granulated sugar
4 oz butter
2 teaspoons vanilla essence

Put the milk into a heavy saucepan and bring slowly to the boil. Add the sugar and butter and heat slowly, stirring all the time, until the sugar dissolves and the butter melts. Bring to the boil and cover the pan with a lid. Boil for 2 minutes and then uncover. Boil steadily for 10 to 15 minutes to 237°F/114°C (soft ball). Take off the heat, stir in the essence and leave for 5 minutes to cool. Beat until the fudge loses its gloss and is thick and creamy. Pour into a greased tin and mark into squares when cool.

VARIATIONS

Cherry. Add 2 oz chopped glacé cherries.
Chocolate. Add 4 oz grated plain chocolate to the milk before cooking.
Coconut. Add 3 tablespoons desiccated coconut.
Fruit and Nut. Add 1 oz currants and 1 oz blanched chopped almonds.
Walnut. Add 2 oz finely chopped walnuts.

SWISS FUDGE

4 oz butter
8 fl oz milk
2 lb granulated sugar
1 small can sweetened condensed milk

Melt the butter slowly in the milk, add the sugar and dissolve over a gentle heat, stirring all the time. When the sugar has dissolved, add the condensed milk and bring slowly to the boil. Stir over a low heat till the mixture turns a light caramel colour and begins to thicken; this takes approximately 20 minutes. Remove the mixture from the heat and beat vigorously until thick, approximately 5 minutes. Pour into a greased tin and leave to cool. When setting, mark the fudge out into small squares. When cold, break into squares.

MARSHMALLOW FUDGE (1)

> 4 oz icing sugar
> 2 oz seedless raisins or chopped nuts
> 4 oz marshmallows
> 2 tablespoons milk
> 2 oz granulated sugar
> 2 oz butter

Mix the icing sugar and raisins or nuts. Melt the marshmallows gently in 1 tablespoon of milk. Leave to cool. Put the remaining milk into a pan with the granulated sugar and butter and heat slowly. Stir all the time until the sugar dissolves and the butter melts, and boil for 5 minutes. Take off the heat and add the melted marshmallow mixture and gradually stir in the icing sugar and raisins or nuts. Mix well and spread in a greased tin. Leave until firm and set.

MARSHMALLOW FUDGE (2)

> 1 lb granulated sugar
> 1 small can evaporated milk
> 3 tablespoons water
> 2 oz butter
> 1 teaspoon vanilla essence
> 8 marshmallows, cut into quarters
> A few hazelnuts

Put the sugar, milk and water into a strong pan. Heat slowly until the sugar dissolves, brushing down the sides with water to remove any sugar crystals. Bring to the boil, stirring frequently, to 237°F/114°C (soft ball). Remove from the heat, add the butter and vanilla essence. Leave the contents of the pan without stirring until lukewarm. Then beat until the mixture holds its shape, add the marshmallows and beat well again. Spread in a greased tin. Place the hazelnuts at spaced intervals over the surface. When firm, cut into squares.

SYRUP FUDGE

    2 tablespoons golden syrup
    3 tablespoons water
    3 oz butter or margarine
    1 lb caster sugar
    1 small can sweetened condensed milk
    Few drops of vanilla essence

Put the syrup, water, butter or margarine and sugar into a heavy saucepan. Heat slowly until the sugar has dissolved. Add the condensed milk, bring to the boil and boil for 10-15 minutes until the mixture is golden brown and reaches 237°F/114°C (soft ball). Take off the heat and beat until thick. Add a few drops of essence and pour into a lightly greased tin. Mark the fudge into pieces with a knife when half set.

RUM RAISIN FUDGE

    1 lb granulated sugar
    2 oz butter
    ¼ pint evaporated milk
    ¼ pint water
    1 teaspoon rum
    4 oz seedless raisins

Put the sugar, butter, milk and water into a large saucepan. Heat gently till the sugar has dissolved and the fat has melted, then bring to the boil. Boil rapidly, stirring, to 237°F/114°C (soft ball). Remove from heat, add the rum and raisins, and beat well until the mixture becomes thick and creamy. Pour into a greased tin. When nearly set, mark into squares.

CAN'T FAIL FUDGE

> 5 fl oz evaporated milk
> 16 marshmallows
> 10 oz granulated sugar
> Pinch of salt
> 2 oz butter
> 6 oz plain chocolate
> Few drops of vanilla essence
> 4 oz chopped walnuts

Put the evaporated milk, marshmallows, sugar, salt and butter into a thick pan. Bring to the boil, stirring well, and boil for 5 minutes. Chop the chocolate into small pieces. Remove the mixture from the heat and stir in the chocolate until melted. Add the vanilla essence and walnuts and pour into a greased tin. Cool until firm and cut into squares.

MAPLE FUDGE

> 8 fl oz maple syrup
> 8 oz caster sugar
> Pinch of salt
> 4 fl oz single cream
> 3 oz chopped nuts

Put the syrup, sugar, salt and cream into a thick saucepan and heat gently, stirring often, until the sugar has dissolved. Bring to the boil and then simmer without stirring to 237°F/114°C (soft ball). Remove from the heat and cool to lukewarm. Beat with a wooden spoon until thick and creamy. Fold in the nuts and pour into a greased tin. Cut into pieces when cold.

NUT FUDGE

    4 oz butter
    8 tablespoons granulated sugar
    ½ teaspoon vanilla essence
    8 tablespoons golden syrup
    1 large tin sweetened condensed milk
    4 oz chopped mixed nuts

Melt the butter in a thick saucepan. Add the sugar and essence and bring very slowly to the boil. Add the syrup and condensed milk and boil until the mixture thickens and turns deep golden brown at 237°F/114°C (soft ball). Cool to lukewarm and then beat with a wooden spoon until thick and creamy. Add the nuts and pour into a greased tin.

CHOCOLATE NUT FUDGE

    1 lb granulated sugar
    ½ pint milk
    2 oz plain chocolate, grated
    1 oz butter
    4 oz chopped mixed nuts
    ½ teaspoon vanilla essence

Put the sugar into a thick saucepan with the milk, chocolate and butter. Heat slowly until the chocolate, sugar and butter have melted. Simmer to 237°F/114°C (soft ball). Take off the heat, cool to lukewarm and then beat with a wooden spoon until thick and creamy. Stir in the nuts and essence and pour into a greased tin.

BLACK TREACLE FUDGE

    1 lb granulated sugar
    4 tablespoons black treacle
    6 tablespoons milk
    2 oz butter

Heat the sugar, treacle and milk in a thick saucepan over a low heat until the sugar dissolves. Boil rapidly to 237°F/114°C (soft ball). Take off the heat and add the butter. Leave until lukewarm, stirring occasionally. Beat until thick and pour into a well-greased tin. Mark into squares when cool. A few chopped nuts are also good in this fudge.

COFFEE NUT FUDGE

    1½ lb granulated sugar
    13 fl oz water
    2 level teaspoons powdered coffee
    2 oz butter
    6 oz chopped walnuts

Before starting to make this fudge it is important to have all the equipment ready, as it sets very quickly. Grease a tin. Boil together the sugar, water, coffee and butter to 237°F/114°C (soft ball), which will take 10-15 minutes. Remove the saucepan from the heat and beat until the mixture becomes fairly creamy and is mid-brown in colour. Very quickly stir in the chopped walnuts and pour immediately into the greased tin. Spread flat with a spatula before the mixture cools. Allow to go cold before cutting.

COFFEE WALNUT FUDGE

    ½ pint evaporated milk
    1 tablespoon fine coffee powder
    1 lb granulated sugar
    1 oz butter
    4 oz coarsely chopped walnuts

Heat the milk gently with the coffee powder until the coffee has blended. Add the sugar and butter and heat gently until the sugar has dissolved. Boil to 237°F/114°C (soft ball). Cool slightly and add the walnuts. Beat until smooth and creamy and pour into a greased tin; mark into squares when nearly set.

CHOCOLATE SYRUP FUDGE

    1 lb granulated sugar
    1/4 pint milk
    1 tablespoon golden syrup
    4 oz plain chocolate, broken
    2 oz butter
    1/2 teaspoon vanilla essence
    1 teaspoon rum

Heat the sugar, milk and syrup gently until the sugar has dissolved. Add the chocolate and stir until it has melted and the mixture is boiling. Cook to 237°F/114°C (soft ball). Take off the heat, add the butter, and cool without stirring. Add the essence and rum and beat until the fudge is thick and loses its shine. Put into a greased tin and mark into squares when cool.

CHOCOLATE FUDGE

    1 lb granulated sugar
    1/2 oz cocoa
    2 oz plain chocolate, grated
    1/4 pint evaporated milk
    1/4 pint water
    2 oz butter
    1/8 teaspoon cream of tartar
    1/2 teaspoon vanilla essence

Stir the sugar, cocoa, grated chocolate, milk and water and add the butter and cream of tartar. Heat slowly until the sugar has dissolved, then boil to 237°F/114°C (soft ball). Add the vanilla essence, cool slightly and beat until smooth and creamy. Pour into a greased tin and mark into squares when nearly set.

SIMPLE CHOCOLATE FUDGE

½ pint milk
1 lb granulated sugar
1 heaped tablespoon cocoa
1 oz butter

Put the milk and sugar into a large thick saucepan and heat very gently until the sugar has dissolved. Add the cocoa and butter and bring the mixture to the boil. Boil gently, stirring well, for 15 minutes, to 237°F/114°C (soft ball). Take the pan off the heat. Beat the mixture well until it starts to thicken and pour into a greased tin. Leave in a cool place to set and then cut into squares.

BRAZILIAN COFFEE FUDGE

1 lb 2 oz soft brown sugar
8 fl oz strong black coffee
2 tablespoons golden syrup
2 oz butter
Few drops of vanilla essence
4 oz chopped Brazil nuts

Mix the sugar, coffee and syrup in a large thick saucepan. Bring to the boil and boil to 237°F/114°C (soft ball). Take off the heat and add the butter without stirring. Cool to lukewarm and add the essence. Beat with a wooden spoon until the mixture loses its gloss. Stir in the nuts and pour into a lightly greased tin. Cut into squares when cold.

FRUIT AND NUT FUDGE

½ pint milk
2 lb granulated sugar
4 oz butter
½ teaspoon vanilla essence
2 oz raisins or sultanas
2 oz blanched almonds

Soak sugar in the milk for 1 hour, then cook very slowly till the sugar dissolves. Add the butter and when melted, bring the mixture to the boil. Simmer steadily to 237°F/114°C (soft ball). Remove from heat, cool slightly, then beat till fudge is thick and creamy. Add essence, fruit and nuts and pour quickly into a well-greased, shallow tin. Mark into squares and cut when cool and set.

AUNT MARY'S TABLET

    1 lb granulated sugar
    Scant ½ pint water
    2 oz butter
    5 tablespoons sweetened condensed milk
    1 teaspoon vanilla essence

Dissolve the sugar in the water. Add the butter and milk and dissolve in the sugar syrup. Bring to boil, and continue to boil, stirring gently, to 237°F/114°C (soft ball). Add the vanilla essence and pour into a greased tin. When setting, mark with a well-oiled knife and break into squares when cold.

WALNUT TABLET

    2 lb soft brown sugar
    ½ pint creamy milk
    1 tablespoon golden syrup
    1 ½ oz butter
    Few drops of vanilla essence
    2 oz chopped walnuts

Put the sugar, milk, syrup and butter into a saucepan. Stir over the heat until the ingredients melt, then boil hard for 10 minutes, to 237°F/114°C (soft ball). Take off the heat and beat until creamy. Flavour with vanilla and chopped walnuts, and pour into a greased tin. Mark into squares as the mixture cools.

GINGER TABLET

    2 lb demerara sugar
    ½ pint water
    1 oz ground ginger

Put the sugar and water into a heavy saucepan and stir over a gentle heat until the sugar has dissolved and the mixture comes to the boil. Remove any scum, and boil to 237°F/114°C (soft ball). Take off the heat, stir in the ginger and keep stirring until the mixture is thick. Put into a greased tin and mark into squares as the mixture cools. Lemon or rose tablets may be made if white sugar is used instead of brown and the appropriate essence substituted for ground ginger.

ALMOND LUMPS

    1 lb soft brown sugar
    2 tablespoons malt vinegar
    ½ teaspoon vanilla essence
    8 oz roughly chopped blanched almonds

Heat the sugar and vinegar gently until the sugar dissolves. Boil to 237°F/114°C (soft ball). Cool and add the essence and roughly chopped almonds. Beat until creamy and drop in small lumps on to a greased tin.

PANOCHA

    1¾ lb brown sugar
    Pinch of salt
    1 tablespoon golden syrup
    1 oz butter
    1 small can evaporated milk
    1 tablespoon water
    ½ teaspoon vanilla essence
    2 oz roughly chopped walnuts

Put the sugar, salt, syrup, butter, milk and water into a saucepan. Cook over a low heat, stirring all the time, until the sugar dissolves. When it has dissolved, boil to 237°F/114°C (soft ball). Cool at room temperature until lukewarm. Add the vanilla essence and beat the mixture until it holds its shape. Add the nuts, and spread quickly in a greased tin. Cool and cut into squares.

OLD-FASHIONED PENUCHE

    1 lb soft brown sugar
    6 fl oz creamy milk
    1 tablespoon golden syrup
    2 tablespoons butter
    1 teaspoon grated orange rind
    Few drops vanilla essence
    4 oz chopped walnuts

Put the sugar, milk, syrup, butter and orange rind into a large, thick saucepan. Stir all the time until the mixture boils, and then boil gently to 237°F/114°C (soft ball). The mixture may look curdled at this stage. Take off the heat and leave to stand without stirring until the bottom of the pan feels lukewarm. Stir in the vanilla essence and the walnuts, and beat with a spoon until the mixture is thick and creamy and loses its gloss. Pour into a greased tin and mark into squares while still warm.

ALMOND CANDY

    6 oz ground almonds
    6 oz caster sugar
    6 oz icing sugar
    2 eggs, beaten
    1 dessertspoon lemon juice
    Few drops vanilla essence
    1 oz blanched almonds
    1 oz halved glacé cherries

Line a tin with waxed paper and then put rice paper on top of this. Put the almonds, caster and icing sugar into a thick saucepan and mix them well. Add the beaten eggs, lemon juice and essence. Cook gently, stirring all the time, for 10 minutes. Add the almonds and cherries and pour into the tin. When cold and firm, cut into bars.

GINGER CANDY

 1 lb soft brown sugar
 1 tablespoon plain white flour
 6 tablespoons water
 ¼ oz ground ginger

Put the sugar into a thick saucepan. Separately, mix the flour and water until creamy and add the ginger. Add this mixture to the sugar and stir well. Boil for 25 minutes and pour into a greased tin. Cut into squares when cold.

MIXED FRUIT CANDY

 2 lb cube sugar
 ½ pint water
 ¼ teaspoon cream of tartar
 1 oz walnut kernels
 1 oz glacé cherries
 1 oz angelica

Put the sugar and water in a thick saucepan and dissolve the sugar slowly over a low heat. Boil for 15 minutes, stirring occasionally. Add the cream of tartar and continue boiling for 10 minutes to 237°F/114°C (soft ball). Meanwhile, chop the walnuts, cherries and angelica into small pieces. Remove the candy from the heat and when it has stopped bubbling, add the nuts and fruit and stir it hard until it becomes thick and opaque. Pour quickly into a greased tin. If the mixture hardens too soon and is not smooth and creamy, heat it gently again, beat it and pour it into the tin. Before the candy sets, mark it into squares with a knife which has been dipped in hot water.

WALNUT CANDY

> 1 lb granulated sugar
> 3 ½ fl oz milk
> ½ oz butter
> 8 fl oz evaporated milk
> 2 oz chopped walnut kernels
> Few drops of vanilla essence

Put the sugar, milk and butter into a thick saucepan and heat gently until the sugar has dissolved. Boil for 15 minutes. Stir in the evaporated milk and boil for a further 15 minutes, stirring all the time, to 247°F/119°C (hard ball). The mixture will have turned pale-coffee colour. Add the chopped walnuts and vanilla essence, beat and pour into a greased tin. Cool and cut into pieces.

COFFEE CANDY

> 1 lb granulated sugar
> ¼ pint milk
> ¼ pint strong black coffee
> 1 tablespoon sweetened condensed milk

Put the sugar, milk, coffee and condensed milk into a heavy saucepan and bring to the boil, stirring very gently all the time. Boil to 237°F/114°C (soft ball), take off the heat and beat until creamy. Pour into a greased tin.

LEMON CANDY

> 1 lb cube sugar
> ½ pint water
> 1 tablespoon lemon essence
> 2 oz butter

Dissolve the sugar in the water over a gentle heat. Boil until the syrup candies round the pan. Take it off the heat and add the lemon essence and butter. Beat until thick and creamy and pour into a greased tin.

BROWN COCONUT CANDY

> 2 lb soft brown sugar
> ½ pint water
> ¼ pint milk
> 8 oz desiccated coconut
> Few drops of vanilla essence

Dissolve the sugar in the water over a gentle heat, then boil until the sugar candies round the edge of the pan. Stir in the milk and coconut and boil for 5 minutes, stirring well. Add the essence, take off the heat and beat until creamy. Pour into a tin rinsed with cold water.

NUT CANDY

> 1 lb granulated sugar
> fl oz water
> 2½ fl oz milk
> 2 oz chopped nuts

Heat the sugar and water gently until the sugar has dissolved. Stir in the milk and boil to 237°F/114°C (soft ball). Take off the heat and stir in the nuts. Beat until creamy and pour into a greased tin.

TREACLE CANDY

> 1 oz butter
> ½ pint milk
> 6 oz black treacle
> 8 oz desiccated coconut

Melt the butter, add the milk and treacle and stir together until the mixture boils. Add the coconut and bring back to the boil. Boil to 237°F/114°C (soft ball) and pour into a buttered dish.

SWEDISH MOLASSES CANDIES

    8 oz granulated sugar
    8 oz black treacle
    2 oz butter
    8 fl oz double cream
    2 oz blanched almonds

Mix the sugar, treacle, butter and cream in a thick saucepan and cook over a low heat, stirring constantly, to 237°F/114°C (soft ball). Chop the almonds and stir into the mixture. Pour into small, paper sweet cases and leave to set.

AMERICAN COCONUT CUBES

    12 oz soft brown sugar
    4 oz desiccated coconut
    4 fl oz milk
    1 tablespoon butter
    Pinch of salt

Put the sugar, coconut, milk, butter and salt into a thick saucepan and stir over low heat until the sugar has dissolved. Bring to the boil and boil to 237°F/114°C (soft ball) stirring all the time. Take off the heat and beat until cool. Pour into a greased tin. Cut into cubes when set.

7 Fondants and Creams

Fondant may be cooked or uncooked. The uncooked variety is simple to make and is therefore particularly suitable for children to prepare without supervision. It will not keep long and soon becomes hard and dry.

Boiled fondant will keep fresh and can be stored for future use. It is best wrapped in greaseproof or waxed paper then placed in a jar with an airtight lid, or in a polythene container, for storage. For short-term storage, the paper-wrapped fondant can be stored under a damp cloth. When it is needed for use, the fondant can be put into the top part of a double saucepan, or in a basin standing in a pan of hot water. It can then be melted over very gentle heat, with a little sugar syrup to thin it down if necessary. It should not be overheated or it will become rough and lose its gloss.

When the fondant has been prepared, it is best left to stand for 2 or 3 hours covered with a damp cloth. If the fondant is to be stored for later use, colouring and flavouring should not be added until it is to be used. It may be used for simple fondants or creams, or used as a coating for glacé fruit or nuts, or it can be combined with marzipan, jelly or nougat to make attractive sweets. Fondant can also be worked into fudges, nougats and candies to give a richer and more creamy mixture.

When the fondant has been cooked, it should be poured on to a wet dish or marble surface and left for 10-15 minutes to cool. To test if it is the correct temperature, put a hand under the dish and the surface will feel warm. When a skin forms round the edges, work the mixture with a wooden spatula or spoon, turning sides to middle and top to bottom until the mixture becomes white and thick. Work the fondant in a small area until it is really firm and opaque. Take it from the slab and knead it until the texture is smooth and even, adding very little stock syrup if necessary.

The colder the fondant before being worked, the finer will be the grain, resulting in a smooth fondant. If the fondant is too hot, it will be 'gritty'. It will take longer to work if very cold and it will not turn so quickly; it is also liable to become hard and crumbly. But this can be put right if the mixture is warmed slightly and a little stock syrup added. 'Grittiness' also results if the sugar has not been properly dissolved in water before boiling.

To colour the fondant and add flavouring, divide the mixture into portions, and add delicate colouring, flavouring appropriately and kneading until the colour is evenly blended. A little cream, evaporated milk or melted butter added just before making up sweets will improve texture and flavour.

Fondants may be shaped by hand or by rolling and cutting, but for a professional finish, they should be moulded in rubber fondant moulds or starch trays. Fondant for rubber moulds should not be hotter than 140°F/60°C when poured in after melting gently. For starch trays, the temperature should be no more than 120°F/50°C and even less for coating. If the fondant is over-heated it will set hard, streaky and dull. If it is too soft, it will not set or turn out of the moulds. A starch tray is made by filling a tray to the top with confectioner's starch or cornflour, which must be dried in a slow oven and sieved, then smoothed down in the tray. Small plaster moulds should be placed about 1½ in. apart to make impressions in the starch. Pour the melted fondant into the impressions with a funnel or a teaspoon, and dust the surface with a little starch or cornflour. When cold and set, put the sweets on a rack and brush off surplus starch.

For coating centres with fondant, use a small baking tray lined with waxed paper, and a thin fork such as a pickle fork. Use thick, cool fondant melted over warm water. Prepare the centres from marzipan, sliced glacé fruit or nuts, forming them into small round or oval shapes, and see they are in a warm room for some time before coating so the fondant does not set on them too quickly when dipping takes place. Drop centres into fondant singly, lifting out carefully with the fork and placing on the waxed paper. Put tiny decorations of glacé fruit, nuts or silver balls on at once.

FONDANT (1)

> ¼ pint water
> 1 lb granulated sugar
> ¼ level teaspoon cream of tartar
> Few drops of colouring and flavouring

Put the water and sugar into a large thick saucepan. Heat gently until all the sugar has dissolved. Bring to boiling point, add the cream of tartar and boil for 10 minutes to 237°F/114°C (soft ball). Have a cup of water and a bristle pastry brush ready to brush down the sides of the pan to prevent crystals forming. Sprinkle a little water on a baking tray and put it on a board. Pour on the hot syrup and leave until a thick skin forms over the surface. Work the mixture quickly with a spatula until it cools and becomes grainy and white. When it is cool enough, knead until it is smooth.

Divide the fondant for colouring and flavouring and deal with a small quantity of fondant at a time. Colour and flavour appropriately (e.g. pink with rose-water; yellow with lemon). While working with small pieces of fondant, put the remainder in a bowl over a saucepan of hot water to keep it soft.

FONDANT (2)

> 12 oz granulated sugar
> ¼ pint water
> 1 teaspoon liquid glucose
> Few drops of colouring and flavouring

Dissolve the sugar in the water over gentle heat. Add the glucose and boil to 237°F/114°C (soft ball). Have a cup of water and a bristle pastry brush ready to brush down the sides of the pan to prevent crystals forming. Sprinkle a little water on a baking tray and put it on a board. Pour on the hot syrup and leave until a thick skin forms over the surface. Work the mixture quickly with a palette knife until it cools and becomes grainy and white. When it is cool enough, knead until it is smooth.

Divide the fondant for colouring and flavouring and deal with a small quantity of fondant at a time. Colour and flavour appropriately (e.g. pink with rose-water; yellow with lemon). While working with small pieces of fondant, put the remainder in a bowl over a saucepan of hot water to keep it soft.

STOCK SYRUP

> 1 lb granulated sugar
> ½ pint water

Dissolve the sugar in the water over gentle heat. Boil to 220°F/105°C (smooth) and skim if necessary. Strain into a wide-mouthed jar which has a glass stopper. Add to fondant as necessary when melting to obtain the right consistency.

UNCOOKED FONDANT*

    1 lb icing sugar
    1/4 teaspoon cream of tartar
    4 tablespoons evaporated milk
    A little white of egg, lightly beaten

Sieve the icing sugar and mix with the cream of tartar. Add the milk and enough lightly beaten egg white to make a pliable paste. Knead very well and wrap in greaseproof paper to mellow for an hour or two before use.

FRUIT FONDANT*

    1 lb uncooked fondant (as above)
    4 oz glacé cherries
    2 oz glacé pineapple
    Few drops of cochineal
    Few drops of raspberry essence
    Few drops of vanilla essence
    A little icing sugar
    Beaten egg white
    A little caster sugar

Divide the fondant into three portions. Colour one portion pink and flavour lightly with raspberry essence. Combine the other two portions, flavour with vanilla and knead in the chopped cherries and pineapple, using a little icing sugar to avoid stickiness. Roll out the pink portion 1/8 in. thick and cut it into two halves. Roll the white portion to the size of one of the pink pieces. Brush each pink portion with a little egg white and sandwich the white fruit portion between them. Roll lightly with a rolling pin dusted with caster sugar, so that the layers stick together. Put into a tin lined with greaseproof paper, and cover with another piece of paper and weigh down well. Next day, cut into small squares.

COCONUT FONDANT*

    1 lb uncooked fondant (as page 67)
    4 oz desiccated coconut
    Few drops of cochineal
    Few drops of raspberry essence
    Few drops of vanilla essence
    A little icing sugar
    Beaten egg white

Knead the coconut into the fondant and divide the mixture into two portions. Colour one half pink and flavour with raspberry essence. Flavour the remainder with vanilla essence. Roll out the two portions to the same size, about 1/4 in. thick, using a little icing sugar to prevent sticking. Sandwich together with a little egg white and press under a weight in a tin lined with greaseproof paper. Cut into small bars the next day.

MAGIC FONDANTS*

    8 oz icing sugar
    2-3 tablespoons sweetened condensed milk

Sift the icing sugar into a bowl and blend in the condensed milk until smooth and creamy. This fondant can be used for various sweets:

1. Flavour with peppermint for peppermint creams. Roll out to 1/4 in. thick and cut into rounds. Leave to set.

2. Roll small quantities into balls, press glacé cherries in them and mould petals made from fondant on the outside.

3. Add flavouring and suitable vegetable colouring. Press into sweet moulds. Leave to set. Remove and serve, or roll out and cut into squares, triangles or crescents.

COCONUT KISSES*

> 8 oz fondant, cooked or uncooked
> 4 oz desiccated coconut
> Few drops vanilla flavouring
> Few drops almond flavouring
> Few drops green vegetable colouring
> Few drops raspberry flavouring
> Few drops cochineal

The fondant can be prepared in advance from one of the basic recipes on pages 65, 66 or 67. Knead all but one tablespoon of the coconut into the fondant; divide the mixture into three parts. Into one work a few drops of vanilla; into the second, a few drops of almond flavouring and green colouring; into the third, a few drops raspberry flavouring and cochineal. Form each batch of mixture into small pointed rolls, using the remaining coconut to help press the soft mixture into shapes.

CHOCOLATE ALMOND CREAMS*

> 2 oz ground almonds
> 2 oz icing sugar
> 1 teaspoon Cointreau
> 1 tablespoon whipped double cream
> 6 oz plain chocolate, broken

Mix the ground almonds and icing sugar together and moisten with the Cointreau. Mix to a very firm paste with the cream. Chill in the refrigerator and form into small olive shapes. Warm the chocolate in a basin over hot water until just melted. Dip the sweets in the chocolate and put on a rack to cool.

PEPPERMINT CREAMS (1)*

> 8 oz icing sugar
> 2 tablespoons sweetened condensed milk
> Few drops of oil of peppermint
> Few drops of green colouring

Sift the icing sugar into a bowl. Add the condensed milk and mix until smooth and creamy. Add a few drops of peppermint oil to flavour, and colour green if liked. Work the flavour and colour evenly through the mixture. Roll out to $\frac{1}{4}$ in. thick and cut into rounds with a small cutter. Leave in a cool place to set.

PEPPERMINT CREAMS (2)*
    1 lb icing sugar
    Few drops of oil of peppermint or peppermint essence
    1 egg white
    2 tablespoons double cream

Sieve the icing sugar and make a well in the centre. Mix a few drops of peppermint oil or essence with the egg white and cream. Add this to the icing sugar to form a stiff paste and knead the mixture thoroughly. Roll out on a board dusted with icing sugar and cut out with small cutters or cut into squares. Put on a wire cake rack and leave overnight to dry.

OPERA CREAMS
    1 lb cube sugar
    $\frac{1}{4}$ pint water
    2 oz powdered glucose
    2 tablespoons single cream
    2 oz icing sugar
    Few drops of colouring and flavouring

Put the sugar, water and glucose into a heavy saucepan and heat gently until the sugar has dissolved. Boil to 237°F/114°C (soft ball). Pour on to a slab and work until white with a wooden spoon or spatula and with the hands. Put the mixture back into the saucepan and add the cream and icing sugar, then stir until mixture is soft and workable. Flavour and colour to taste and put on the slab. Form into a square and roll out 1 in. thick, using a little icing sugar and keeping the mixture smooth and even.

Leave until cold and set and cut into squares with a very sharp knife.

ORANGE AND LEMON CREAMS*

    1 lb icing sugar
    1 stiffly beaten egg white
    Grated rind and juice of 2 oranges or lemons
    Few drops orange or yellow colouring (optional)

Sieve the icing sugar and work in the stiffly whipped egg white and grated rind of the oranges or lemons. Strain the fruit juice. Add the juice gradually and mix to a stiff paste, adding a little colouring if liked. Sprinkle a board with icing sugar and put the paste on to it. Knead well and work with the hands. Roll out ¼ in. thick and cut into small shapes. Put on waxed paper to dry in a warm room for 12 hours before packing.

COFFEE CREAMS*

    1 lb icing sugar
    4 teaspoons coffee powder
    2 oz butter
    2 tablespoons milk

Mix the icing sugar and coffee powder carefully. Melt the butter and warm the milk slightly. Mix the butter and milk and gradually stir into the icing sugar. Turn on to a board and knead with a little icing sugar until smooth. Roll into small balls and flatten them slightly. Leave in a cool place until firm.

PEPPERMINT WAFERS*

    1 lb icing sugar
    1 teaspoon peppermint essence
    2 oz butter
    2 tablespoons milk

Mix the icing sugar and essence. Melt the butter and slightly warm the milk. Work them into the icing sugar and knead on a board with a little icing sugar until smooth. Roll out to ⅛ in. thick and cut into 1½ in. rounds with a biscuit cutter. Leave until cool and firm. These wafers are delicious if dipped into melted plain chocolate.

COCONUT KISSES*

> 8 oz fondant, cooked or uncooked
> 4 oz desiccated coconut
> Few drops of cochineal

The fondant may be prepared from one of the basic recipes on pages 65, 66 or 67.

Warm the fondant by standing it in a pan of hot water. Stir in the coconut and mix well. Divide the mixture in halves and colour one half pale pink. Put the mixture into small pyramids in paper sweet cases. Sprinkle a little desiccated coconut over each one and leave to harden.

FONDANT ROLL*

> 8 oz fondant, cooked or uncooked
> 2 oz ground almonds
> Few drops of vanilla essence
> Few drops of coffee essence
> Few drops of raspberry essence
> Few drops of cochineal
> 1 egg white
> 2 oz almonds, chopped, blanched and toasted

The fondant can be prepared from one of the basic recipes on pages 65, 66 or 67.

Knead the fondant well and add the ground almonds. Work the

fondant until it is smooth and creamy, and divide into three portions. Leave one portion white and flavour with vanilla. Flavour the second portion with coffee. Flavour the third portion with raspberry essence and colour it pink. Roll out the three portions ¼ in. thick keeping them in strips as near the same size as possible. Brush the edges of the white portion with egg white and sprinkle chopped, blanched and browned almonds down the centre. Press on the pink fondant. Brush egg white on the edge of this and sprinkle on the remaining almonds. Cover with coffee fondant and press well together. Form the fondant into a roll like a Swiss roll and brush the edge with egg white. Press closely together until firm. Wrap in greaseproof paper and leave for 6 hours. Cut into slices when hard.

FONDANT FRUITS
Use pieces of crystallised ginger, cubes of glacé pineapple or other glacé fruit, or bunches of raisins or grapes. Dip the fruit in liquid fondant and put into paper cases to dry.

8 Marzipan

Marzipan or almond paste may be made uncooked or cooked, and is useful for a variety of attractive sweets. Marzipan can be stored for weeks, wrapped in waxed paper in a polythene bag in a cool dry place, and if it gets dry, it can be kneaded with a little egg white or stock sugar syrup to make it more pliable.

Marzipan can be flavoured and coloured appropriately to be rolled into balls, formed into fruit, or rolled out for cutting into squares or fancy shapes, or used for stuffing fruit and nuts. Marzipan can also be coloured by painting with vegetable colouring, but these sweets should not be packed with mixed sweets as the colour may rub off.

UNCOOKED MARZIPAN*

    8 oz icing sugar
    8 oz ground almonds
    1 lightly beaten egg
    ½ teaspoon vanilla essence
    Squeeze of lemon juice

Sieve the sugar and work in the almonds, lightly beaten egg, essence and just enough lemon juice to make a stiff dough. Knead lightly to a smooth texture and use as required. A little almond essence or orange-flower water can be used instead of vanilla essence.

COOKED MARZIPAN

    1 lb cube sugar
    ¼ pint water
    Pinch of cream of tartar
    12 oz ground almonds
    A few drops almond essence
    1 lightly beaten egg or 2 egg whites

Cooked marzipan is easy to knead and mould and can be shaped into fruit or novelty shapes for cake decoration. Sweets made from this marzipan keep well. Put the sugar into the water and leave it to soak for 1 hour, then dissolve the sugar over gentle heat. Bring to the boil, add the cream of tartar, and cook until the syrup reaches 237°F/114°C (soft ball). Take off the heat and stir in the ground almonds and essence. Cool and mix in the lightly beaten egg or egg whites. When the mixture is cold, turn on to a board or table which has been sprinkled with icing sugar and leave overnight. Knead the marzipan and model into fruit or other shapes, colouring small quantities as needed.

MARZIPAN FRUITS*

    10 oz ground almonds
    6 tablespoons sweetened condensed milk
    Few drops of almond essence

Put the ground almonds in a bowl and work in the milk with a wooden spoon. Add a few drops of almond essence to taste. Use to make fruit shapes, e.g. oranges, lemons, apples, pears, etc., painting them with edible colourings.

CHOCOLATE MARZIPAN*

    3 oz caster sugar
    3 oz icing sugar
    2 oz plain chocolate, broken
    1 tablespoon hot water
    6 oz ground almonds
    1 small egg
    Squeeze of lemon juice
    Few drops of vanilla essence

Mix the caster and icing sugar together very well. Melt the chocolate in the water over a pan of hot water. Stir into the sugar together with the almonds. Beat the egg lightly and add it to the chocolate mixture with the lemon juice and essence. Knead well to a smooth paste and lightly roll into a rectangle. Cut into squares, roll in a little caster sugar and leave to dry.

HONEY MARZIPAN*

    4 oz ground almonds
    1 tablespoon thick honey
    Few drops of almond essence
    Few drops of colouring (optional)

Mix the almonds to a firm paste with the honey, adding a few drops of almond essence. Add a few drops of colouring if liked.

The mixture can then be divided into green, pink and yellow portions for making mixed sweets. Work the marzipan until smooth. Use for stuffing dates or for sandwiching nuts. Make Neapolitan sandwiches with three coloured portions. Try rolling small balls of marzipan and dipping them in melted plain chocolate.

FRUIT MARZIPAN

    1 lb cube sugar
    Pinch of cream of tartar
    2½ fl oz water
    8 oz ground almonds
    1 tablespoon fruit purée

Put the sugar, cream of tartar and the water into a heavy saucepan and heat gently until the sugar dissolves. Boil to 247°F/119°C (hard ball). Remove from the heat and stir in the almonds and the fruit purée. Cook over a very low heat until the mixture is thick and does not cling to the sides of the pan. Turn out on to a slab and cool. Roll out ¼ in. thick and cut into shapes. The marzipan may be lightly coloured to match the flavour of the fruit purée. Apricot and raspberry purée are very good for this sweet, and the purée should be thick and strongly flavoured. If very pretty sweets are to be made, ice the marzipan with thin glacé icing and sprinkle with finely chopped pistachio nuts.

STUFFED DATES*

    1 box (24) dates
    2 oz marzipan, cooked or uncooked
    2 oz desiccated coconut

The marzipan can be prepared from one of the basic recipes on page 75.

Split each date along the top and remove the stone. Divide the marzipan into 24 equal pieces, and press a piece of marzipan into each date. Put the coconut into a paper or polythene bag and drop each date in separately. Shake gently until it is covered in coconut. Put each filled date into a small paper case.

STUFFED WALNUTS*
> Marzipan, cooked or uncooked
> Green colouring
> Walnut halves

The marzipan can be prepared using one of the basic recipes on page 75.

Colour the marzipan green by working in a small amount of edible green colouring with the hands. Divide the paste into small even-sized pieces. Roll into balls and press a half walnut on each side. Arrange in paper cases.

CARAMEL FRUIT AND NUTS
> 8 oz walnut kernels, or dates or prunes (or a mixture)
> 8 oz ground almonds
> 8 oz caster sugar
> 2 egg yolks
> Few drops of almond essence
> Lemon juice
> 1 lb cube sugar
> ¼ pint water
> Few drops of colouring (optional)

If walnuts are being used, toast them in the oven for 10 minutes. Use high-quality dates or prunes and remove the stones carefully without damaging the fruit. Mix the ground almonds, caster sugar, egg yolks and almond essence and add a squeeze of lemon juice. Work to a smooth paste and colour lightly if liked, either green or pink. Divide the almond paste into pieces about the size of a small nut and sandwich pieces between two walnut halves, or use pieces to stuff dates or prunes. Leave on a wire rack until the almond paste is cool and firm.

Put the cube sugar, water and a squeeze of lemon juice into a thick saucepan and boil quickly without stirring until the syrup turns golden brown. Take the pan from the heat and stand it at once in a bowl of cold water. Dip in the nuts and fruit one at a time, working quickly. Put on to an oiled slab or dish. When cold, place the nuts and fruit in paper cases.

GLACÉ MARZIPAN

> 6 oz marzipan, cooked or uncooked
> 8 oz granulated sugar
> 6 tablespoons water
> Large pinch of cream of tartar

The marzipan can be prepared from one of the basic recipes on page 75.

Form the marzipan into 16 small balls and put a cocktail stick into each one. Leave until the next day to harden. Stir the sugar into the water and dissolve it completely over low heat. Add the cream of tartar and boil gently until golden brown. Dip the balls quickly into the syrup and leave to set on an oiled plate. Put into small sweet papers to serve. Eat fairly quickly while the glaze is still crisp.

MARZIPAN FRUIT AND VEGETABLES*

These are best made with cooked marzipan (see recipe, page 75), which is easier to mould. Colour marzipan delicately, mixing colours if necessary. Extra colour can be painted on with a fine paint brush after modelling. After hardening shapes overnight, glaze them with a little gum arabic and sugar softened in water and painted on with a brush.

Acorns Colour marzipan green and form into acorn shapes. Brush a little egg white over the rounded end and dip in cocoa or melted chocolate. Stick a slice of chocolate in the other end to make a dark point.

Apples Colour marzipan rich green, adding a little yellow. Form into a circle and depress one end slightly with a skewer. Use a clove at the end. Give a rosy 'bloom' by painting on a little red colouring

Apricots Colour with yellow and red to make the correct pale orange. Roll into balls and mark a groove down one side. Mark one or two 'blemishes' by making a small dent in the surface and filling it with cocoa or drinking-chocolate powder.

Bananas Colour yellow and mould round pieces. Lengthen them and slightly taper, then bend into shape. Pinch natural ridges along the banana. Paint with a little chocolate brown and green, using a real fruit as an example.

Carrots Colour orange with a red tinge. Mould into correct shape, pointing at one end. Mark round circles with a knife and rub a little cocoa into them. Use angelica for stalk.

Lemons Colour bright yellow and form round shapes, lengthening them slightly at one end. Roll over fine nutmeg grater to give a rough finish and pinch slightly at one end.

Oranges Colour orange and form into rounds, then flatten slightly. Roll over fine nutmeg grater to give a rough finish and stick a clove in one end.

Peaches Colour orange with yellow added to achieve the correct shade. Form into balls and mark a line down one side with a knife. Paint on 'blush' with a fine brush and red colouring. Dust over peach with a piece of cotton wool dipped in cornflour.

Pears Colour with green, mixing in yellow and brown for the correct shade. Roll in rounds, then roll one end to form pear shapes. Paint lightly with chocolate brown or red for shading. Put a clove in the bottom and an angelica stalk at the top.

Potatoes   Use plain marzipan and roll between the hands into round and oval shapes. Mark 'eyes' with a small skewer, and dust with drinking-chocolate powder.

Strawberries   Colour light red and mould into balls. Taper at one end and flatten the sides. Colour some granulated sugar red beforehand, and roll the strawberries in this. Use angelica for stalks, or mould hulls and stalks from green marzipan.

Turnips   Use egg white only to make marzipan. Form into rounds, and taper at one end. Use angelica for stalks and paint a little green colouring at the top.

9 Gelatine Sweets

Powdered gelatine is simple to use as it dissolves easily in hot water. It is important never to add gelatine granules to boiling liquid. Always dissolve it first by mixing with cold water, then stand the bowl in a pan of hot water until the mixture becomes syrupy.

Gelatine may be used to make the usual sweetmeats, such as mashmallow and Turkish delight, but it is also advantageous to use it in such dishes as coconut ice and fudge, where the thickening of the mixture relies upon beating after boiling. In this case, the gelatine helps to prevent a coarse, granular texture from developing. When making peppermint creams, it replaces the use of egg white and acts as a binding as well as a setting agent. Always ensure that the mixture is left for the correct length of time to obtain perfect setting.

Jellies are best finished by rolling them in equal quantities of sifted icing sugar and cornflower. They should be stored by packing closely in the same mixture. Jellies may also be slightly moistened and then coated with caster sugar, or they can be dipped in melted chocolate.

MARSHMALLOWS

    1 tablespoon cooking oil
    10 oz granulated sugar
    1 dessertspoon liquid glucose
    ½ pint water
    1 envelope (or 3 teaspoons) gelatine
    ¼ teaspoon vanilla essence
    1 egg white
    Few drops of cochineal
    1 oz icing sugar ⎱ sieved together
    1 oz cornflour ⎰

Oil thoroughly a 7 in. square tin. Put the sugar, glucose and ¼ pint water into a saucepan. Heat gently until the sugar is dissolved. Bring to the boil and continue to boil for about 5 minutes, or until when a little of the mixture is dropped into cold water it forms a soft ball (237°F/114°C). Meanwhile, dissolve the gelatine in the remaining ¼ pint hot water. Pour it into the boiling syrup and whisk thoroughly. Continue to cook for about 2 minutes. Add the vanilla essence. Allow to cool. Whisk the egg white until stiff. Add the ~~the~~ mixture and whisk until light, fluffy and thick, at the same time adding sufficient cochineal to colour pink. Pour into the oiled tin. Stand in a cool place for several hours or until firm to the touch. Spread the sieved icing sugar/cornflour on to a sheet of greaseproof paper. Turn the marshmallow on to it and cut into squares, tossing each piece in the icing sugar/cornflour mixture. Leave until firm. Pack into a container with the remaining cornflour/icing sugar.

VARIATION: Omit the cochineal. Roll the marshmallow squares

in toasted coconut instead of icing sugar and cornflour. Marsh-mallows may also be flavoured with rose-water or orange-flower water.

TURKISH DELIGHT (1)

½ pint water
1 oz gelatine
1 lb granulated sugar
Rind and juice of 1 orange
Juice of 1 lemon
Cornflour
Icing sugar

Put ¼ pint of the water into a small pan with the gelatine. Stir over a gentle heat until dissolved, then boil for 3-4 minutes. Put the sugar into a pan with the remaining ¼ pint water, dissolve, stirring over a low heat, then bring to the boil. Cool slightly, add the dissolved gelatine and simmer gently, stirring all the time for 20 minutes. Remove from the heat. Add the orange rind and orange and lemon juice. Cover and leave to stand for 10-15 minutes. Strain into a rectangular tin, approximately 6 in. × 4 in. rinsed in cold water. The mixture should be about ½ in. thick. Leave to set. When set cut into squares. Roll in cornflour and then in icing sugar. Pack in a box lined with wax paper, thickly sprinkled with icing sugar.

TURKISH DELIGHT (2)

1 tablespoon cooking oil
½ pint hot water
1 oz gelatine
1 lb granulated sugar
¼ level teaspoon citric acid
1 tablespoon rose-water
Few drops of cochineal

1 oz icing sugar
1 oz cornflour } sieved together

Oil thoroughly a 3 in. × 7 in. loaf tin. Put the water into a pan and sprinkle on the gelatine. Stir in the sugar and citric acid. Place over a gentle heat and stir until the sugar and gelatine have dissolved. Boil and continue to boil over a moderate heat for 20 minutes. Add the rose-water and sufficient cochineal to colour pink. Leave the mixture to cook for 15 minutes. Pour into the oiled tin. Leave to set for 24 hours. Spinkle the sieved cornflour and icing sugar mixture on to a sheet of greaseproof paper. Turn the mixture on to this and cut into cubes, using a sharp knife. Completely coat the cubes in the cornflour/icing sugar. Store in a container packed with the remaining cornflour/icing sugar.

HONEY TURKISH DELIGHT

Rind and juice of 1 large orange
Rind and juice of 1 small lemon
1 lb granulated sugar
½ pint water
1 oz gelatine
Few drops of orange colouring
1 tablespoon clear honey
2 oz icing sugar
1 oz cornflour

Remove the rind of the orange and lemon very thinly. Put into a large thick pan with the sugar, the strained juice of the orange and lemon, and half the water. Dissolve the sugar completely and bring slowly to the boil. Put the gelatine into the rest of the water in a bowl and put this into a pan of hot water until the gelatine becomes syrupy. Add to the sugar syrup and boil gently for 20 minutes, stirring often. Cool for 20 minutes, then stir in the orange colouring and honey, and strain into a shallow baking tin which has been rinsed in cold water. Leave to set overnight. Sift the icing sugar and cornflour together on a sheet of grease-proof paper. Cut the jelly into squares with a knife dipped in hot water. Toss in the sugar mixture and leave for a few hours to dry. Store in an airtight tin. Nuts can be added to the Turkish delight if liked.

Peppermint Delight. Use green colouring and oil of peppermint for flavouring.

Rose Delight. Use pink colouring and rose-water or rosehip syrup for flavouring.

CHOCOLATE TURKISH DELIGHT

    Turkish delight (as recipe 1, page 84)
    8 oz melted chocolate or chocolate-flavoured cake coating

Prepare the chocolate but make quite sure it is as cool as possible before use. Stand each piece of Turkish delight on a fork and dip it into the chocolate to give an even coating. Lift out of the chocolate and carefully remove the excess chocolate on the top rim of the container. Place on lightly oiled greaseproof paper and immediately put in a cool place until the chocolate is set. Store in a cool, dry place.

ISTANBUL DELIGHT

    1 lb granulated sugar
    1 ½ pint water
    ¼ level teaspoon tartaric acid
    3 oz cornflour
    7 oz icing sugar
    2 level tablespoons honey
    5 teaspoons lemon juice
    1 ½ teaspoons rose-water
    1 oz almonds (blanched, chopped and toasted)

Few drops of cochineal
2 oz sieved icing sugar

Put sugar and ¼ pint water into a saucepan. Heat very slowly until the sugar has dissolved. Boil to 237°F/114°C (soft ball) and add the tartaric acid. Blend the cornflour with the remaining water, and add the icing sugar. Bring to the boil stirring to prevent lumps from forming. Boil and beat until thick and clear. Add the syrup gradually. Boil for 25 minutes, stirring continually. Add the honey, lemon juice, rose-water and nuts. Pour half the mixture into a buttered 7 in. square tin. Colour the remainder pink and pour on top. Leave for 24 hours. Cut into small squares. Roll in icing sugar.

ORANGE DELIGHT
    1 lb granulated sugar
    ½ pint water
    Rind and juice of 2 small oranges
    1 oz gelatine
    1 tablespoon honey
    Few drops of orange colouring
    1 teaspoon rum
    Icing sugar
    Cornflour

Put the sugar and ¼ pint water into a saucepan and dissolve the sugar completely over gentle heat. Add the orange rind which has been peeled very thinly and cut into very small strips. Bring this to the boil. Dissolve the gelatine in the remaining water over gentle heat and then add it to the other saucepan. Bring to the boil and boil gently for 20 minutes, stirring all the time. Add the strained juice of the oranges, cover and leave to stand without heating, for 15 minutes. Add the honey, a few drops of colouring and the rum. Skim and strain into a tin rinsed in cold water.

Leave until the next day when set. Cut into squares and toss in a mixture of icing sugar and cornflour.

BASIC JELLIES
   1 lb granulated sugar
   ¼ pint water
   ¼ level teaspoon cream of tartar mixed with 1 tablespoon
      water
   2 teaspoons gelatine
   2½ fl oz cold water

Dissolve the sugar in the water and strain the syrup. Add the cream of tartar, boil to 237°F/114°C (soft ball) and remove from the heat. Add the gelatine softened in 2½ fl oz of water, stir very gently over a low heat for 1 minute only, then remove.

TO FLAVOUR AND COLOUR THE JELLIES

Fruit jellies: Add to the above ½ level teaspoon of citric acid dissolved in 1 tablespoon of water, also 1 teaspoon of fruit flavouring and suitable colouring. Stir gently until evenly distributed and then pour into a 7 in. square tin greased with butter and leave overnight to set firmly.

Crème de menthe jellies: Add to the above syrup 1 good teaspoon of peppermint essence or ¼ teaspoon oil of peppermint and colour green. Pour into a 7 in. square greased tin and leave overnight to set.

To finish off the jellies, sprinkle the top with caster sugar. Loosen by hand and lift out on to a slab in one piece. Cut into even strips with a long, sharp knife and dip the cut edge into caster sugar at once. Cut the strips neatly into squares or oblongs and again dip the cut edges, at once, into sugar.

NOTE: If preferred, crème de menthe jellies may be coated in a mixture of 2 parts sieved icing sugar and 1 part cornflour.

CRÊME DE MENTHE JELLIES (1)

    1 ½ tablespoons gelatine
    ½ pint water
    8 oz cube sugar
    Few drops of green colouring
    Few drops oil of peppermint
    Icing sugar
    Cornflour

Dissolve the gelatine a little of the water and heat over boiling water until the mixture is syrupy. Dissolve the sugar in the remaining water by heating gently. Add the gelatine liquid and bring to the boil, stirring gently. Cook for 15 minutes, still stirring. Take off the heat and add enough green colouring to give a pale jade colour. Put on the heat again until the mixture boils. Cool slightly, and then stir in a little oil of peppermint. Pour into a tin rinsed with cold water, and leave to set for 24 hours. Turn out, cut in squares and roll in a mixture of icing sugar and cornflour.

CRÊME DE MENTHE JELLIES (2)

    2 envelopes (or 6 teaspoons) gelatine
    ½ pint cold water
    8 oz granulated sugar
    Pinch citric acid
    1 teaspoon peppermint essence
    Few drops of green colouring
    Caster sugar

Dissolve the gelatine in a little of the water and heat over boiling water until the mixture is syrupy. Place the remaining water and sugar in a saucepan, stir till dissolved, and add the citric acid and gelatine. Bring to the boil and boil for 20 minutes. Remove from the heat, cool, add the peppermint essence and colour a bright green; mix thoroughly together. Pour into a lightly buttered pan and leave for 24 hours. Cut into squares and roll in caster sugar.

LEMON PASTILLES

  1 pint of unsweetened apple purée
  12 oz granulated sugar
  1 ½ oz gelatine
  2 ½ fl oz water
  Few drops of lemon essence
  Few drops of lemon colouring
  Cornflour
  Caster sugar

Cook the apple purée and sugar together until very thick. In a separate bowl, stir the gelatine into the water and stand the bowl in a pan of hot water until the gelatine is syrupy. Stir this into the apple mixture together with the lemon essence and colouring. Pour into a tin rinsed with cold water. When the mixture is set, cut it into shapes and toss in a mixture of cornflour and sugar.

ORANGE PASTILLES

  4 oz granulated sugar
  ¼ pint orange juice
  1 oz gelatine
  6 tablespoons powdered glucose
  Caster sugar

Dissolve the sugar in gently warmed orange juice and cool. Put the gelatine into a bowl with 1 tablespoon water and stand the bowl in a pan of hot water until the gelatine is syrupy. Stir the gelatine and glucose into the orange juice and mix well. Pour into a tin rinsed with cold water. Leave until firm, then turn out and cut into squares or rounds. Toss in caster sugar.

RAINBOW JUBES

  2 envelopes (or 6 teaspoons) gelatine
  ½ pint water
  8 oz granulated sugar

1 tablespoon lemon juice
Few drops of cochineal
Few drops of green colouring
Few drops of yellow colouring
Icing sugar or desiccated coconut

First, dissolve the gelatine in a little cold water and heat over boiling water until syrupy. Place the ½ pint of water and the sugar in a saucepan with the gelatine. Boil for 20 minutes. Remove from the heat and when cool add the lemon juice. Divide into three parts: colour the first part red with cochineal; the second, yellow; and the third, green. Put one part into a lightly buttered pan; when firm enough add the second part, and when this is firm, add the third part. Leave for 24 hours at least. Cut into squares and roll in icing sugar or coconut.

FRENCH JELLIES

4 envelopes (or 12 teaspoons) gelatine
7 fl oz cold water
2 lb granulated sugar
½ pint boiling water
1 saltspoon citric acid
Few drops of yellow colouring
Few drops of lemon essence
Few drops of cochineal
Few drops of vanilla essence
Icing sugar

Dissolve the gelatine in 7 fl oz of cold water and heat over boiling water until syrupy. Dissolve the sugar and citric acid in boiling water. Add the gelatine. Boil for 25 minutes, stirring all the time one way. Remove scum as it forms on the surface. Divide the mixture and pour into two shallow dishes rinsed in cold water. Colour one yellow and flavour with lemon. Colour the other with cochineal and flavour with vanilla or other flavouring. Leave for

24 hours. Cut into strips and roll in icing sugar. Then cut into squares and roll again in icing sugar.

DATE PRALINES

    2 envelopes (or 6 teaspoons) gelatine
    ½ pint water
    8 oz granulated sugar
    8 oz icing sugar
    8 oz chopped dates
    Few drops vanilla essence
    Icing sugar and cornflour sieved together

Mix the gelatine with a little cold water and heat over boiling water until syrupy. Put ½ pint water and the granulated sugar in a saucepan with the gelatine and bring to boiling point. Boil for 10 minutes then leave to cool. Add the icing sugar and whisk until thick and white. Flavour with vanilla. Add the dates and mix thoroughly. Place in lightly buttered pans. Leave for 24 hours. Cut into squares and roll in a mixture of icing sugar and cornflour.

VARIATIONS
Cherry Pralines. Use chopped glacé cherries.
Fig Pralines. Use chopped figs.
Ginger Pralines. Use chopped preserved ginger
Nut Pralines. Use chopped nuts.

MOONSHINE BIFFS

    2 envelopes (or 6 teaspoons) gelatine
    ½ pint water
    8 oz granulated sugar
    8 oz icing sugar
    Few drops of vanilla essence
    Desiccated coconut

Mix the gelatine with a little water and heat over boiling water until syrupy. Place ½ pint of water and the granulated sugar in a saucepan with the gelatine and stir until dissolved. Boil for 8 minutes, then allow to cool. Add the icing sugar and vanilla essence and whisk until thick and white. Wet a plate or sandwich tin and pour on the mixture. Leave for 24 hours. Cut into small squares. Roll in desiccated coconut or icing sugar.

FONDANT

> 2 teaspoons gelatine
> 8 oz granulated sugar
> ¼ pint water
> ⅛ teaspoon cream of tartar
> Few drops of flavouring essence
> Few drops of colouring

Mix the gelatine with a little of the water and heat over boiling water until syrupy. Place all the ingredients except flavouring and colouring in a saucepan over a gentle heat. When dissolved bring to boiling point without stirring and boil for 5 minutes or to 237°F/114°C (soft ball). Remove from heat; leave until luke-warm. Add flavouring. Beat until thick and creamy. Turn on to a plate and knead until soft and smooth. Colour while warm. When firm, cut into desired shapes or use for the following confections:

Date Creams. Remove stones from dates, fill with fondant.
Ginger Creams. Add small pieces of preserved ginger to the mixture while beating
Peppermint Creams. Flavour the mixture with a few drops of peppermint and colour a delicate green.
Prune Creams. Remove stones from prunes, fill with fondant.
Walnut Creams. Place pieces of fondant between halves of walnut or work chopped walnuts into mixture while beating.

PEPPERMINT CREAMS

⅛ pint water
1 envelope (or 3 teaspoons) gelatine
12 oz icing sugar
Few drops of green colouring
Few drops of oil of peppermint or peppermint essence
1 tablespoon cornflour ⎫
1 tablespoon icing sugar ⎭ sieved together

Dissolve the gelatine in the water and heat over boiling water until syrupy. Leave to cool slightly. Sieve the icing sugar into a bowl. Stir in sufficient liquid gelatine to form a stiff paste. Knead until the mixture becomes smooth, working in green colouring and oil of peppermint to taste. Roll out to ⅛ in. thick, using the mixture of icing sugar and cornflour to prevent sticking. Cut into 1 in. diameter circles with a small biscuit cutter. Place on a tray dusted with remaining icing sugar/cornflour. Allow to dry for several hours. Store in a cool, dry place.

CHOCOLATE PEPPERMINT CREAMS

Peppermint creams (as above recipe)
4 oz melted dark chocolate or chocolate-flavoured cake covering

Prepare the peppermint creams. Brush off any excess icing sugar/ cornflour mixture. Dip half of each cream into the melted chocolate. When the chocolate has hardened, store in a cool, dry place.

VARIATION: Place the plain peppermint creams on a tray. Brush off any excess icing sugar/cornflour mixture. Pipe fine lines of melted chocolate across the top of each. When the chocolate is dry, store as above.

RUSSIAN CARAMEL

4 oz butter
1 lb brown sugar
1 large tin sweetened condensed milk
1 teaspoon gelatine
1 teaspoon vanilla essence

Place the butter in a saucepan over low heat and when melted, add the sugar, milk and gelatine. Cook slowly until the mixture leaves the side of the saucepan, stirring occasionally to prevent burning. Add essence. Pour into a lightly buttered pan. When firm cut into squares.

COCONUT ICE

1 teaspoon gelatine
1 lb granulated sugar
¼ pint milk
2 oz desiccated coconut

Mix the gelatine with a little water and heat over boiling water until syrupy. Boil together the sugar and milk for 10 minutes. Add the gelatine and allow to cool. Beat until the mixture is white and thick. Stir in the coconut. Turn into a buttered tin. The mixture may be divided before pouring into the tin, colouring one half pink. When firm, remove from the tin and cut into squares.

MILK CHOCOLATE FUDGE

1 teaspoon gelatine
1 lb granulated sugar
½ pint milk
3 dessertspoons drinking chocolate
2 oz butter
½ teaspoon vanilla essence
Pinch of cream of tartar
Pinch of salt

Mix the gelatine with a little water and heat over boiling water until syrupy. Put all the ingredients into a saucepan. Gradually bring to the boil, stirring all the time. Continue to boil but without stirring to 237°F/114°C (soft ball). Beat until creamy. Pour into a buttered tin. Mark into squares. When cold, cut into squares and store in a tin or screw-topped jar.

PERSIAN DELIGHT

  2 lb granulated sugar
  2 pints water
  12 oz powdered glucose
  7 oz cornflour
  ½ teaspoon citric acid powder
  1½ oz gelatine

Mix 1½ lb sugar and 1¼ pints water and heat gently until the sugar dissolves. Bring to the boil and stir in 8 oz glucose. Mix the cornflour with ½ pint water and add to this the boiling syrup, stirring until thick, keeping the heat low. Add the citric acid dissolved in 1 dessertspoon water, and cook slowly for 30 minutes. Dissolve the remaining sugar and half the water and bring to the boil in a separate pan. Add the remaining glucose and boil to 237°F/114°C (soft ball). Pour in a steady stream into the main batch of syrup. Stir the gelatine into the remaining water in a bowl and stand it in a pan of hot water until the gelatine is syrupy. Stir into the syrup mixture. Add any flavouring and pour into a tin rinsed with cold water. Leave until set, then cut in squares and toss in a mixture of icing sugar and cornflour. For a most delicious flavour, substitute rose-water for the water and add a pinch of powdered cardamom.

10 Chocolate

Sweets made with chocolate are always popular, but they need a little extra care in preparation. Couverture chocolate, for professional work, is not readily obtainable, but high-quality, plain, block chocolate, chocolate chips, or cake-covering chocolate can be easily used with good results. The chocolate can be used as the basis of such sweets as truffles, can bind together fruit and nuts, or can be used to coat a variety of centres. Nougat, caramels, fondants, jellies, marzipan and fudge all make excellent 'centres', and they should be made in advance, left to firm up and kept in a warm room until coated.

Chocolate work should be done on a dry, medium-warm day. Humidity affects chocolate, so other cooking should be avoided at the same time to ensure that there is no steam or dampness in the kitchen. Heat the chocolate very gently in the top of a double saucepan or in a basin over hot water. This water should not be kept boiling or it will overheat the chocolate. If the pan is removed from the heat as soon as the water boils, the chocolate will remain warm and workable for some time. If the chocolate becomes too cold, dipped chocolates will not be glossy: if it is hot and thin, the coating will not stay on the centres and drying will take longer. Centres should be dipped one at a time (use a fine skewer or pickle fork), any surplus chocolate shaken off, and the chocolates put on to a cold marble slab, which will help them to set quickly with a glossy finish. If this is not available, use a sheet of foil or wax paper or a clean baking tray. Chocolates may be marked with a pattern with a fork, or decorated with silver balls, crystallised violets, etc.

MOULDED CHOCOLATE

Tin or plastic moulds are available for making Easter eggs, and for figures suitable for Christmas-tree decorations or for cakes. Use cake-covering chocolate for these and heat it over hot water until it has just melted. Make sure the moulds are clean and pour in the chocolate. For figure moulds, fill these completely. For Easter eggs, half fill the moulds, then tilt them so that the chocolate runs evenly to the edge of the mould all round. When the chocolate is cold and can be released from the moulds, do not touch the outer glazed surface more than necessary. Join two halves of an egg by lightly touching the rims on a warm flat tin, just enough to soften them slightly so they can be pressed together.

CHOCOLATE TRUFFLES*

    8 oz plain chocolate
    1 heaped tablespoon caster sugar
    2 oz sugar
    2 tablespoons rum or cream
    1 egg yolk
    Cocoa or chocolate vermicelli etc, for coating

Break the chocolate into small pieces and melt it in a basin over hot water. Remove from the heat and stir in the sugar, butter, rum or cream and egg yolk. Beat until thick and cool. Shape into small balls and leave to dry. Roll in cocoa, chocolate vermicelli, hundreds-and-thousands or desiccated coconut.

CHOCOLATE CREAM TRUFFLES*
        2 oz plain chocolate, broken
        3 dessertspoons double cream
        1 teaspoon vanilla essence
        8 oz icing sugar
        Chocolate vermicelli

Put the chocolate into a basin over hot water and leave until melted, stirring occasionally. Add the cream and essence and gradually work in the icing sugar. Turn on to a plate and leave about 1½ hours until cool enough to handle. Roll into small balls and toss in chocolate vermicelli.

CHOCOLATE RUM TRUFFLES*
        4 oz plain chocolate
        2 oz butter
        1 tablespoon rum
        2 egg yolks
        1 oz ground almonds
        1 oz stale cake crumbs
        8 oz icing sugar
        Drinking-chocolate powder

Break the chocolate into small pieces and melt it with the butter in a basin over hot water, stirring occasionally. Add the rum and egg yolks, and gradually work in the ground almonds, cake crumbs and icing sugar. Mix well and turn on to a plate. Leave until cool and firm, which takes about 1½ hours. Roll into small balls and toss in drinking-chocolate powder.

VARIATIONS

Sherry, Whisky or Liqueur. Substitute sherry, whisky or a fruit-flavoured liqueur for the rum.

Orange. Leave out the rum, but add finely grated rind of 1 small orange and 1 tablespoon orange juice.

RUM TRUFFLES*

    8 oz plain chocolate
    1 tablespoon sweetened condensed milk
    ½ teaspoon rum
    Cocoa

Break the chocolate into small pieces and melt it in a saucepan over hot water. Remove from the heat and add the milk and rum. Stir well and then beat until cool. Shape into small balls and toss them in cocoa powder. Leave to set firmly.

COFFEE TRUFFLES*

    4 oz butter
    6 oz icing sugar
    8 oz plain chocolate, broken
    Few drops of coffee essence
    Chocolate vermicelli or cocoa

Cream the butter and icing sugar. Melt the chocolate over hot water; allow to cool. When the chocolate is nearly cold, beat it into the butter mixture, together with coffee essence. Shape into small balls and roll in chocolate vermicelli or cocoa.

CHOCOLATE BRITTLES

    2 oz almonds
    6 oz caster sugar
    4 oz plain chocolate
    Cocoa or powdered drinking chocolate

The almonds need not be blanched. Dissolve 2 oz sugar over low heat until liquid. Add the almonds and boil together until light brown. Pour on to an oiled tin and leave until cold. Crush the mixture to a powder. Break the chocolate into small pieces and melt it in a bowl over hot water. Remove from heat and mix with remaining sugar. Stir in the almond powder and form into small balls. Leave to harden and roll in a little cocoa or powdered drinking chocolate.

SUGAR BALLS*

    4 oz plain chocolate, roughly broken
    3 tablespoons single cream
    2 oz caster sugar
    16 sponge finger biscuits, finely crushed
    2 tablespoons sherry

Place the chocolate in a basin over hot, not boiling, water. Stir until smooth. Remove from heat. Stir in the cream and sugar. Add the crushed sponge finger crumbs and the sherry. Blend well. Leave the mixture in a cool place overnight to stiffen. Form heaped teaspoons of the mixture into balls, then roll them in caster sugar. Store in a screw-topped jar.

CHESTNUT NIBBLES

    1 lb chestnuts
    2 oz butter
    4 oz plain chocolate, grated
    2 oz vanilla sugar

Prick the chestnuts and place in boiling water. Cook until the shells can be easily removed. Remove the shells and cook the chestnuts for a further 20-30 minutes until tender. Drain and sieve. While still hot, beat in the butter, 2 oz of the chocolate and the vanilla sugar. Line a 7 in. square tin with greaseproof paper and grease with butter. Spread the chestnut mixture in the tin and leave in the refrigerator for several hours until set hard. Stamp out the mixture with a small round cutter, approximately 1 in. in diameter, and roll the pieces in the remaining grated chocolate. Serve in paper cases.

CHOCOLATE CHERRIES*
> Glacé cherries
> Plain chocolate, roughly broken

Put the cherries on to cocktail sticks. Soften the chocolate in a bowl over hot water. Dip the cherries into the chocolate and stick the free end of the cocktail sticks into an apple. Leave until the chocolate sets. Maraschino cherries are delicious for this, but they must be very well drained and dried on kitchen paper before dipping.

CHOCOLATE CRUNCH*
> 4 oz plain chocolate
> 1 oz glacé cherries
> 1 oz angelica
> 1 oz sultanas
> 1 oz raisins
> 1 oz walnuts

Break the chocolate into small pieces and melt it in a bowl over hot water. Chop the cherries, angelica, sultanas, raisins and walnuts roughly and blend into the chocolate. Drop spoonfuls of the mixture into paper sweet cases and leave until set. Store in a tin.

CHOCOLATE LIQUEURS
> 24 maraschino cherries
> 4 tablespoons brandy
> 8 oz plain cake-covering chocolate

2 oz granulated sugar
2 tablespoons water
2 oz butter
2 oz icing sugar

Cover the cherries with the brandy and leave to soak for a few hours. Take some paper sweet cases and use two together so that they are firm. Break the chocolate into small pieces and melt half of it in a bowl over hot water. Brush it fairly thickly inside the sweet cases to cover the sides and bases completely. Leave to set. Drain the brandy from the cherries and put one cherry in each chocolate case. Dissolve the sugar in the water and boil to a thick syrup. Add half the drained brandy, stirring gently, and cool. Cover the cherries with this syrup. Cream the butter and icing sugar and flavour with the remaining brandy and pipe this on to the liqueurs. Chill in a refrigerator until firm. Melt the remaining chocolate (reserving a little for later use), allow it to cool and just before it sets pour it over the liqueurs to seal the tops. Before this layer sets, cover with a little finely grated chocolate. Leave until cold and set and remove from paper cases.

WHIPPED CREAM WALNUTS
Milk or plain cake-covering chocolate, broken
Thick whipped cream
Walnut halves

Line some egg cups with kitchen foil, turning it down a good way round the outside. Melt the chocolate over hot water and, using a very narrow palette knife or a teaspoon, coat the foil with a good layer of melted chocolate. Allow to cool. Repeat this three times in all to give a strong casing. When the chocolate is set, fill with cream and put a walnut half on top. Cover with more melted chocolate to seal the cases. When set, remove from the egg cups and peel off the foil. Turn upside down and fix a walnut on top of each with a little melted chocolate.

AFTER DINNER MINTS*
 6 oz milk or plain cake-covering chocolate
 4 oz icing sugar
 Few drops of oil of peppermint

Break the chocolate into small pieces and melt it in a bowl over hot water. Paint a thick layer of the chocolate on to waxed paper and leave to set. Mix the icing sugar, a few drops of peppermint oil and a little water to a stiff paste. Spread this mixture over the chocolate layer and leave to set. Paint another thick layer of chocolate on top and leave to set. Cut in squares.

CHOCOLATE GINGERBALLS*
 4 oz plain cake-covering chocolate
 1 ½ oz crystallised ginger

Break the chocolate into small pieces and melt it in a basin over hot water. Cut the ginger into very fine shreds. When the chocolate has just melted, stir in the ginger lightly until blended. Put small spoonfuls of the mixture on greaseproof paper and leave to harden.

CHOCOLATE COCONUT BARS
 8 oz milk or plain cake-covering chocolate
 2 oz butter
 1 small tin sweetened condensed milk
 4 tablespoons icing sugar
 8 oz desiccated coconut

Break the chocolate into small pieces and melt it in a bowl over hot water. Line a Swiss-roll tin with greaseproof paper and cover with half the melted chocolate. Leave to cool. Melt the butter, milk and sugar in a pan and add the coconut. Mix well and spread this over the chocolate layer. Cover with the remaining melted chocolate. Cut into fingers when cold.

11 Fruit and Nuts

Candied and glacé fruit, sugared nuts and crystallised flowers all make delicious additions to the range of home-made sweet-meats. They are particularly attractive to serve with coffee after a meal, together with peppermint creams and Turkish delight. They are also useful to keep in store to decorate cakes, puddings and ices.

CANDIED FRUIT

Use fresh cherries, oranges, pears, pineapple or stoned fruits. Canned fruits are also very good and are easy to process.

To begin, good quality fresh fruit should be gently cooked in water until just tender. Canned fruit should be drained from its syrup. Fresh fruit should be processed initially with a syrup made from ½ pint water and 6 oz granulated sugar for each pound of fruit. When using canned fruit, allow 1 lb fruit to ½ pint liquid from the canning syrup and any necessary water to cover.

Heat the syrup and use it to cover the fruit completely, keeping the fruit submerged with a saucer over the liquid if necessary. Leave to stand for 24 hours. Drain off the syrup, add 2 oz sugar to it and dissolve. Boil and pour over the fruit. Repeat this process twice more, adding 2 oz sugar each time. On the fifth day, add 3 oz sugar, and boil for 4 minutes. Leave for 2 days. Repeat the process and leave the fruit to soak for 4 days. Drain off the syrup and put the fruit on a wire rack (such as a cake rack) to drain and dry off in a very cool oven or a warm airing cupboard for about 3 days. Store in boxes lined with waxed paper in a cool, dark, dry place. The candied fruit may also be finished in two ways:

Crystallised. Dip each piece of candied fruit quickly into boiling water. Drain well and roll each piece in caster sugar.

Glacé. Make a new syrup with 1 lb granulated sugar and ¼ pint water, and boil for 1 minute. Pour some of the syrup into a cup. Dip each piece of fruit in boiling water for 20 seconds, then dip into the syrup. Put on a rack to dry. Keep the remaining syrup warm over hot water and when the syrup in the cup becomes cloudy, discard it and put in some of the remaining 'clean' syrup. Turn the fruit frequently as it dries off.

CANDIED ORANGE PEEL

> Peel of 3 oranges
> 4 oz cube sugar
> 1 teaspoon water
> Granulated sugar

Cut the peel in strips, cover with water, then boil until the white pith can be scraped off with a spoon. Make a syrup of the cube sugar and water. Cook the peel in this until transparent, when it will have absorbed nearly all the syrup. Lift the pieces with a fork, roll them in granulated sugar, and leave them on a wire tray until cool and dry. Store in an airtight glass jar.

CANDIED GOOSEBERRIES

    1 lb large ripe gooseberries
    1 lb granulated sugar
    ½ pint water
    Caster sugar

Use berries which are sound and firm. Boil the sugar and water together to a thick syrup. Put in the gooseberries and simmer for 10 minutes without breaking them. Leave in the syrup to get cold. Boil up again and then put the gooseberries in a sieve to drain off. Dip each berry into caster sugar, then put on to a wire cake rack and leave to dry in a cool oven, 250°F/120°C (Gas Mark ½) for 6 hours. Pack in tins with greaseproof paper between the layers.

CANDIED PLUMS

    1 lb large ripe eating plums
    1 lb granulated sugar
    ½ pint water

Take the stones from the plums, damaging the fruit as little as possible. Boil the sugar and water together until it drops in beads from a spoon. Drop in the plums and simmer until they look transparent. Lift them out, drain off the syrup and put them on to flat dishes. Leave for 24 hours and then boil them again in the syrup. Lift out and put on to a wire cake rack. Dry at 250°F/120°C (Gas Mark ½) for 6 hours. Pack in tins with greaseproof paper between the layers.

MARRONS GLACÉ

    1 lb chestnuts
    1 lb granulated sugar
    ¼ pint water
    ½ teaspoon vanilla essence

Slit the chestnut shells with a sharp knife, but do not cut into the nuts. Boil the nuts for 20 minutes and skin them while still warm. Dissolve the sugar in the water over low heat and then bring to the boil. Add the chestnuts and the essence and boil hard for 10 minutes. Drain the chestnuts on a wire rack. Leave for 24 hours. Boil the syrup again and return the nuts. Simmer until thickly coated with syrup. Drain on a rack for 24 hours before packing.

CRYSTALLISED ANGELICA

Select young stems and stalks of angelica in April. Cut into 4 in. or 5 in. lengths and place in a glass or crockery vessel. Pour over them a boiling solution of 1 pint water and ¼ lb salt. Cover and leave for 24 hours. Lift out, drain on a wire drainer, peel and wash in cold water. Make a syrup of 1½ lb granulated sugar and 1½ pints water and boil for 10 minutes. Place the angelica in the boiling syrup for 20 minutes; lift out and drain for 4 days on a wire drainer. Reboil again for 20 minutes in the same syrup. Allow to cool in the syrup, lift out and drain for 3 or 4 days. Dust with sugar and store in airtight jars.

CRYSTALLISED ORANGES

    3 oranges
    8 oz granulated sugar

Peel the oranges and segment them without breaking the thin skins. Place the segments on a baking sheet on a wire tray and warm them slightly to dry the skins. Put the sugar into a saucepan and heat very gently until it has completely melted, looks clear, and movement almost ceases. Remove the pan from the heat and pour the syrup over the orange quarters covering the whole surface of the fruit. Repeat until all the syrup has been used. Allow to cool and remove from the wire rack when the sugar coating has hardened. Dredge with caster sugar, and serve in paper sweet cases.

ICED ORANGES

>2 egg whites
>1 lb caster sugar
>6 small juicy oranges

Whisk the egg whites to stiff peaks. Add the sugar gradually, beating well for about 10 minutes until the mixture is stiff. Skin the oranges and remove all the pith. Put a thread through the centre of each one. Dip the oranges into the sugar mixture and tie them to an oven rack. Dry at 250°F/120°C (Gas Mark ½) for about 4 hours until the sugar is crisp and dry. Be sure that the oven is not too hot or the oranges will colour.

FROSTED FRUITS

>Selection of fruits, e.g. black and green grapes, oranges and
>   tangerines
>Egg whites
>Caster sugar

Wash the grapes and dry well. Peel the oranges and tangerines and divide into segments. Whisk the egg whites stiffly. Dip each piece of fruit into the egg white and then into the caster sugar. Put the coated fruit on to a cake rack to dry. Serve in sweet cases or arrange attractively as a centre piece for the table.

GLACÉ FRUITS

>Selection of fruit, e.g. black and green grapes, oranges and
>   tangerines
>8 oz cube sugar
>¼ pint water
>2 teaspoons powdered glucose or pinch of cream of tartar

Use of a sugar-boiling thermometer is recommended for this recipe.

Make sure the fruit is quite dry. Dissolve the sugar in the water, bring to the boil and add the glucose (or cream of tartar dissolved in a little water). Boil rapidly to 290-300°F/145-150°C, i.e. just before the sugar changes colour. Stop the boiling by dipping the bottom of the pan in cold water. Have an oiled slab or plate ready, and when the syrup is still, dip each fruit in it, using a dipping fork or long thin skewer. Put the fruit at once on the slab or plate and leave to set. When the sugar is hard put the fruit in small paper cases for serving.

APRICOT JUJUBES

1 lb dried apricots
2¼ lb granulated sugar
Icing sugar

Soak the apricots in water for 24 hours. Put them through a mincing machine twice then place them in a pan with the granulated sugar. Cook gently for 1 hour, stirring often to prevent sticking. Pour into a shallow tin rinsed with cold water. When cold, cut into pieces and roll in icing sugar.

FRUITY COCONUT BITES

4 oz dates
4 oz raisins
3 oz walnuts
4 oz desiccated coconut
2 oz preserved ginger
2 oz candied peel
2 oz figs
1 small can sweetened condensed milk

Chop the fruit and nuts. Mix together all the ingredients reserving half the coconut for later use. Form the mixture into small balls and roll in the remaining coconut. Place on a greased baking tray and bake in a moderate oven, 375°F/190°C (Gas Mark 5), until golden brown, about 5-10 minutes. Cool on a cake rack.

FRUIT AND NUT BALLS*

    8 oz cooking dates
    6 oz seedless raisins
    8 oz dried figs
    4 oz walnuts
    1 teaspoon grated orange rind
    1 tablespoon orange juice
    Icing sugar or chopped nuts, for coating

Put the dates, raisins, figs and walnuts through a mincer, using a coarse blade. Add the orange rind and juice and mix until well blended. Shape into balls about 1 in. in diameter. Roll in a little icing sugar or finely chopped nuts.

HONEY-CANDIED WALNUTS

    12 oz granulated sugar
    Pinch of salt
    2 oz honey
    4 fl oz water
    Few drops of vanilla essence
    12 oz walnut kernels

Put the sugar, salt, honey and water into a thick saucepan, and bring to the boil. Boil to 237°F/114°C (soft ball), stirring often. Take off the heat and add the essence and walnuts. Stir until creamy, and turn into a tin lined with waxed paper, separating the walnuts as much as possible. Divide up when cold.

SPICED WALNUTS

    8 oz granulated sugar
    Pinch of salt
    1 teaspoon cinnamon
    ½ teaspoon nutmeg
    ½ teaspoon ground cloves
    4 fl oz water
    8 oz walnut kernels

Put the sugar, salt, spices and water into a thick saucepan and boil to 237°F/114°C (soft ball), stirring often. Take off the heat and stir in the walnuts. Stir until creamy and turn into a tin lined with waxed paper, separating the walnuts as much as possible. Divide up when cold.

BUTTERED NUTS
    2 oz nuts
    8 oz demerara sugar
    2 oz butter
    ¼ pint water
    ¼ teaspoon cream of tartar

Walnuts, brazils, almonds and hazelnuts are all suitable for this recipe. Brush a tin with oil and put the nuts on it about 2 in. apart. Heat the sugar, butter, water and cream of tartar gently until the sugar dissolves. Heat to 280°F/140°C (soft crack). Pour a teaspoon of the toffee over each nut and leave to set.

APRICOT PASTE
    Ripe apricots
    Granulated sugar

Take the stones from the apricots and cook the fruit with as little water as possible, just enough to prevent sticking. When tender, put through a fine sieve and weigh the pulp. Mix the pulp with an equal weight of sugar, then heat and stir until all the moisture has evaporated and the mixture is dry. Roll the paste on a sheet of paper sprinkled with caster sugar; leave to dry in the sun or in an open oven. The paste should be leathery so that it can be rolled up.

REDCURRANT OR BLACKBERRY PASTE
    2 lb redcurrants or blackberries
    Granulated sugar
    ½ pint water

Heat the currants or berries in water until they burst and are soft. Strain through a jelly bag and weigh the juice. Mix the juice with an equal quantity of sugar, then heat slowly, stirring all the time, until the mixture is thick and dry. Put the paste into a baking tin and sprinkle with caster sugar. When cold and hard, cut into pieces with a knife, dip each piece in caster sugar and store in a wooden box lined with greaseproof paper.

QUINCE PASTE
    Quinces
    Granulated sugar
    Icing sugar

Do not peel or core the quinces but cut them into small pieces. Barely cover with water and simmer until very soft. Sieve and weigh the pulp, then mix with an equal weight of sugar. Put the mixture into a thick pan and stir over a low heat until it dries and leaves the sides of the pan clear. Cool slightly and then roll out ½ in. thick on a board dusted with icing sugar. Stamp out rounds and leave them to dry, turning often, until they are the texture of leather. Dust with icing sugar and store in tins. *Apple paste* and *pear paste* may be prepared in the same way. The mixture can be dried on the rack of a cooker or in a cool airing cupboard.

CRYSTALLISED FLOWERS
Primroses, violets, polyanthus, roses, carnation petals, forget-me-nots, mimosa, cowslips, sweet peas and fruit blossoms are suitable for crystallising. Flowers which come from bulbs should not be eaten. The flowers should be crystallised in a solution of gum arabic crystals and rose or orange-flower water. Allow 3 teaspoons crystals to 3 tablespoons rose water, and leave in a screw top jar for 2 or 3 days, shaking sometimes, until the mixture is a sticky glue. A small, soft paint brush is needed to paint the flowers. Large

flowers should be taken apart and the petals reassembled when needed. The petals must be completely coated, or bare spots will shrivel and not keep. A little vegetable colouring may be added to the solution, but this must be very delicate to remain natural looking. When the flowers have been sugared, they should be dried for about 24 hours until crisp and dry. They are best stored in the dark.

CRYSTALLISED MINT LEAVES
    Fresh mint leaves
    Egg white
    Granulated sugar

Use fresh green mint and well-shaped leaves. Beat the egg white stiffly and coat both sides of the leaves. Coat each leaf with sugar and put them on a wire rack covered with wax paper. Stand the rack in a warm place until the leaves are dry. Store in a tin between layers of waxed paper. Use this method also for rose and carnation petals.

12 Honey

Honey gives a delicious flavour to many sweets, and little is needed to give this flavour—a proportion of about one-sixth of the total sugar content is the usual quantity. Honey is also useful in that it helps to avoid crystallisation.

QUICK HONEY TREATS
>   2 lb cube sugar
>   ¼ pint water
>   2 oz clear honey
>   7 fl oz single cream
>   ¼ oz butter
>   Few drops of strawberry, lemon or vanilla essence
>   Few drops of colouring

Place the sugar in a heavy-based pan with the water and stir over low heat. Stir in the honey, cream and butter and boil to 280°F/140°C (soft crack). Quickly stir in flavouring essence and colouring and pour into a greased tin. Leave to set and then cut into small squares.

HONEY DATES*

Wash dates and remove stones. Fill the cavities with honey mixed with chopped nuts (walnuts, brazils, etc.) or desiccated coconut.

GREEK SWEETS

2½ oz stoned dates
2 egg whites
6 oz caster sugar
1 level tablespoon honey
9 oz ground almonds

Cut the dates into small pieces. Beat together the egg whites, sugar and honey until the mixture is foamy. Fold in the dates and almonds. Place in small heaps on rice paper and bake at 350°F/180°C (Gas Mark 4) for about 15-20 minutes until golden brown.

HONEY MALLOW CRUNCHIES

4 oz marshmallows
2 tablespoons honey
Grated rind of 1 small lemon
Grated rind of ½ orange
2½ oz lightly crushed breakfast cereal—cornflakes, rice crispies, etc.
1 oz raisins

Melt the marshmallows with the honey in a bowl over a pan of boiling water. Stir gently together. Remove from heat and add

lemon and orange rind, crushed cereal and raisins. Mix well
together. With slightly wet hands shape the mixture into small
balls and place each ball in a paper sweet case. Leave to set in
a cool place.

HONEY CHOCOLATE FUDGE

    12 oz demerara sugar
    8 fl oz evaporated milk
    2 oz plain chocolate, chopped
    ¼ teaspoon salt
    2 oz honey
    2 oz butter
    4 oz nuts

Mix the sugar, evaporated milk, chocolate and salt in a large thick
saucepan. Bring to the boil and boil for 5 minutes. Add the honey
and boil to 237°F/114°C (soft ball). Add the butter and leave
the mixture to cool slightly. Beat with a wooden spoon until
creamy, add the nuts, and pour into a greased tin. Mark into
squares when cool and cut when set.

HONEY WALNUT FUDGE

    1 lb caster sugar
    1 oz plain chocolate, chopped
    1 small can evaporated milk
    2 tablespoons honey
    1 oz butter
    4 oz walnuts, chopped

Boil the sugar, chocolate, and evaporated milk made up to just
under ½ pint with water, for 5 minutes. Add the honey and boil
to 237°F/114°C (soft ball). Add the butter and the nuts and beat
until creamy. Pour into a greased tin. Mark into squares before
the fudge sets and cut when firm.

HONEY DELIGHT (1)

    1 lb granulated sugar
    1¼ pints water
    ¼ teaspoon cream of tartar
    3 oz cornflour
    7 oz icing sugar
    2 teaspoons rose-water
    2 oz clear honey
    Few drops of pink food colouring
    ½ oz cornflour   ⎞
    ½ oz granulated sugar ⎠ mixed together

Put sugar in a heavy pan with ¼ pint water and stir over low heat until all the sugar has dissolved. Bring to the boil and continue to boil, without stirring, to 237°F/114°C (soft ball). Remove from the heat, stir in the cream of tartar and leave aside. Put the cornflour and icing sugar in a large pan with 1 pint water and bring to the boil, stirring continuously. Allow to boil for 2 minutes then lower the heat and pour on the sugar syrup gradually, beating well with a wooden spoon. Return to the boil, lower heat and simmer for 30 minutes, stirring. Add the rose-water and honey and mix well. Pour half the mixture into a lightly greased shallow 7 in. square tin. Add colouring to remaining mixture and pour over the mixture in the tin. Leave until cold. Dip a sharp knife in icing sugar and cut the mixture into 1 in. bars. Coat the bars with the cornflour/sugar mixture. Leave for several hours then cut into 1 in. squares. The pieces may be coated in cornflour/sugar again if desired.

HONEY DELIGHT (2)

    ¼ pint water
    1 oz (or 3 teaspoons) gelatine
    4 oz honey

1 teaspoon lemon juice
4 oz granulated sugar
Icing sugar
Cornflour

Soak the gelatine in a little of the water. Boil the remaining water
and add all the ingredients, except the icing sugar and cornflour.
Stir to dissolve the sugar and gelatine and continue boiling for
10 minutes. Pour into a shallow tin rinsed with cold water. When
the jelly is set, cut into squares and dip into a mixture of icing
sugar and cornflour to prevent the squares sticking together.

HONEY FUDGE (1)

2 oz butter
4 tablespoons water
2 tablespoons clear honey
1 lb granulated sugar
8 tablespoons sweetened condensed milk

Put the butter, water, honey, sugar and milk into a heavy saucepan and stir over a low heat until the sugar dissolves. Bring to the
boil and boil for 10 minutes to 237°F/114°C (soft ball). Cool to
lukewarm, beat well and pour into a greased tin.

HONEY FUDGE (2)

8 oz honey
2 lb granulated sugar
4 oz butter
1 medium tin sweetened condensed milk
¼ pint milk

Stir all the ingredients together in a large thick saucepan. Bring
to the boil and heat to 237°F/114°C (soft ball). Take off the heat

and beat hard with a wooden spoon until the mixture thickens. Pour into a greased tin and cut into squares when cool.

HONEY APPLES
        6 small apples
        5 oz honey
        Pinch of cream of tartar

Wipe the apples and put each one on to a wooden skewer or lolly stick. Put the honey into a thick pan and bring it to the boil. Add the cream of tartar and continue boiling to 247°F/119°C (hard ball). Dip in the apples quickly, turning them to coat them completely. Put the apples on a greased plate, or stand them the other way up in a jam jar to cool.

HONEY KISSES*
        1 oz candied peel
        2½ oz blanched almonds
        2 teaspoons honey
        Icing sugar

Chop the peel very finely. Grate the almonds. Mix the peel and almonds together and stir in the honey. Form into small balls and roll them in icing sugar. Leave to dry for 24 hours.

HONEY NUT BALLS*
        2 oz hazelnuts
        1 oz plain chocolate
        1½ oz caster sugar
        2 tablespoons honey
        Grated rind of ½ lemon

Grate the hazelnuts, reserving a spoonful for later use. Grate the chocolate. Mix together the nuts, chocolate, sugar, honey and lemon rind. Form into small balls and roll in the remaining grated nuts.

HONEY TOFFEE

    ¼ pint water
    10 oz butter
    4 oz honey

Put the water, butter and honey into a heavy saucepan and heat gently until the butter has melted. Boil to 237°F/114°C (soft ball). Pour into a greased tin. Mark in pieces as the mixture cools. Wrap the toffees in waxed paper.

HONEY PUFF

    3 tablespoons honey
    5 tablespoons granulated sugar
    4 tablespoons water
    ½ oz butter
    ½ teaspoon malt vinegar
    ½ teaspoon bicarbonate of soda

Put the honey, sugar, water, butter and vinegar into a saucepan and heat slowly, stirring until the sugar dissolves and the butter melts. Bring to the boil, cover and boil for 2 minutes. Uncover and boil without stirring for 5 minutes to 280°F/140°C (soft crack). Take off the heat, add the bicarbonate of soda and quickly pour into a small greased tin. Break in pieces when cold and set. Eat on the day this toffee is made as it quickly goes sticky.

13 Old-fashioned Favourites

Many old-fashioned sweets have disappeared from the shops now that manufacturers have to cope with standard weights, special wrappings and items which have to be distributed nationally and appeal to the widest possible range of customers. The old favourites are remembered with nostalgia, always asked for on sweet stalls at bazaars and fêtes. Most of them are very easy to make, and it doesn't matter a bit if they look thoroughly home-made.

SIMPLE COCONUT ICE*

    6 tablespoons sweetened condensed milk
    9 oz icing sugar

6 oz desiccated coconut
A drop of cochineal

Mix together the condensed milk and icing sugar. Stir in the coconut (the mixture should be very stiff) and divide into two parts. Tint one half of the mixture pale pink with cochineal. Shape the mixture into two identical bars and press firmly together. Dust a tin or plate with icing sugar and leave the coconut ice on this until firm. Cut up into bars or squares.

COCONUT ICE

1 lb granulated sugar
¼ pint milk
4 oz desiccated coconut
A drop of pink colouring

Grease lightly a shallow tin. Put the sugar and milk into a thick saucepan, and heat until it boils, stirring all the time with a wooden spoon. Boil gently for 15 minutes to 237°F/114° (soft ball). Take off the heat and beat in the coconut for 2 minutes. Pour half the mixture into the tin and spread it evenly. Add a few drops of the pink colouring to the remainder and pour it into the tin. Leave to set and cut into squares or bars. It is better to use a heavy enamel pan for coconut ice, as an aluminium pan can sometimes give it a greyish tint.

CHOCOLATE COCONUT ICE

1 lb granulated sugar
¼ pint milk
1 tablespoon cocoa
2 oz desiccated coconut

Put the sugar, milk and cocoa into a thick saucepan. Stir well and boil for 5 minutes. Remove from the heat and stir in the coconut. Beat for 2 minutes and pour into a tin rinsed in cold water. Cut into squares or bars when cold.

TOFFEE APPLES (1)

    1 lb small eating apples
    1 lb demerara sugar
    ⅓ pint water
    3 oz butter
    1 dessertspoon powdered glucose

Wipe the apples well, remove the stalks and spear the apples at the stalk end with wooden sticks. Put the sugar and water into a thick pan and heat slowly until the sugar dissolves. Add the butter and glucose and boil hard to 280°F/140°C (soft crack), which will take about 15 minutes. Dip the apples and put them on a buttered tray until hard, or stand them the other way up in a jam jar (this will avoid the formation of a thick layer of toffee at the base and will give the apples a professional look). Heat up the toffee again and dip the apples a second time. Leave on the tray or in the jar until cold. Wrap in waxed paper when they are cold and set.

TOFFEE APPLES (2)

    8 red apples
    1 lb granulated sugar
    4 oz butter
    2 tablespoons water

Remove the stalks of the apples and insert a stick in each stalk end. Put the sugar, butter and water into a pan and allow the sugar to dissolve slowly over a low heat. Boil the toffee to 280°F/140°C (soft crack). Dip the apples into the toffee, keeping the sticks clear, then dip in cold water and place on greased paper. Eat immediately, as they go sticky on keeping.

PEPPERMINT HUMBUGS (1)

  1 lb demerara sugar
  ¼ pint water
  2 oz butter
  3 drops oil of peppermint
  Pinch of cream of tartar

Put the sugar, water, butter, oil of peppermint and cream of tartar into a heavy saucepan and boil to 280°F/140°C (soft crack). Take off the heat, cool for 2 minutes and pour on to an oiled slab. As soon as the mixture is cool enough to handle, pull into long strips. Divide the mixture and pull half of it until it becomes much paler than the other half. Twist the two halves together and cut into short pieces.

PEPPERMINT HUMBUGS (2)

  1 ½ tablespoons golden syrup
  1 lb demerara sugar
  ¼ pint water
  1 oz butter
  Pinch cream of tartar
  ½ teaspoon oil of peppermint

Place the syrup, sugar, water, butter and cream of tartar in strong pan. Cover, dissolve quickly and bring to the boil (no stirring after boiling). Boil rapidly for 3 minutes. Remove the lid, brush round the sides of the pan with a brush dipped in cold water, boil to 280°F/140°C (soft crack). Pour on to an oiled slab. When cool, pour the oil of peppermint over. Oil hands slightly, fold toffee sides to middle, and pull into an even roll. Cut off 'cushions' with scissors and place on a greased table top or tin.

ACID DROPS

> 1 lb granulated sugar
> 1/4 pint water
> 1/2 teaspoon cream of tartar
> 6 drops lemon juice
> 1 teaspoon tartaric acid
> Icing sugar

Dissolve the sugar in the water and add the cream of tartar. Boil until the mixture becomes slightly yellow. Add the lemon juice. Pour on to a marble slab and work in the tartaric acid with a knife. When the mixture is cool enough to handle, cut it into strips and then into small pieces. Form these into small flat balls and dust them with a little icing sugar.

PEANUT BRITTLE

> 2 tablespoons peanuts, shelled
> 8 oz granulated sugar
> 2 tablespoons water
> 1/2 oz butter
> Few drops of vanilla essence
> 1/4 teaspoon bicarbonate of soda

Rub the peanuts in a clean cloth to take off their skins. Put the sugar into a thick saucepan and dissolve the sugar over a low heat without stirring. When the sugar has completely melted, turn up the heat and boil quickly until the syrup turns pale gold. Add the peanuts to the syrup with the butter and essence. Stir quickly, take off the heat, and stir in the bicarbonate of soda. Pour immediately into an oiled tin. Break into pieces when cold.

KENDAL MINT CAKE

> 1 lb granulated sugar
> 1/4 pint milk
> Oil of peppermint

Boil the sugar and milk, stirring all the time, to 237°F/114°C (soft ball). Beat the mixture for 2 minutes until cloudy, then boil to 247°F/119°C (hard ball). Take off the heat, add a few drops of peppermint oil and stir until the mixture is thick. Pour into a tin rinsed with cold water.

This sweet can also be made with soft brown sugar. It is a great energy-giving sweet and is often carried by climbers (slabs were taken up Everest). It is very good to finish an open-air picnic after swimming or walking.

LEMON SHERBET*

    2 lb caster sugar
    ½ oz citric acid
    Few drops of lemon essence

Put the caster sugar into a liquidiser goblet and blend into fine crystals but not powder. Stir in the citric acid and lemon essence mixing well. Leave to dry and put into a screw-top bottle to store. To serve as a drink, add 2 teaspoons to a glass of water.

HONEYCOMB

    1 oz butter
    6 oz granulated sugar
    2 tablespoons golden syrup
    2 tablespoons water
    ½ teaspoon malt vinegar
    1 teaspoon bicarbonate of soda

Put the butter, sugar, syrup and water into a heavy saucepan and stir over a low heat until the sugar has dissolved. Boil to 280°F/140°C (soft crack). Take off the heat and stir in the vinegar and the bicarbonate of soda. The mixture will rise up in a froth in the pan. Pour at once into a greased tin. Break into pieces when cold. Eat quickly because this toffee does not keep well.

COTTAGE CANDY

        8 oz demerara sugar
        6 oz golden syrup
        4 oz butter
        3 tablespoons water
        1 dessertspoon powdered glucose

Put all the ingredients into a heavy saucepan and stir over a low
heat until the sugar has dissolved. Boil to 247°F/119°C (hard ball)
and pour on to a buttered plate. When the mixture is cool enough
to handle, dust the hands with a little flour and caster sugar and
work the toffee into a ball. Pull it out into long strands and
knead them in again. Continue doing this until it is pale-coloured.
Pull into long sticks and twist into walking-stick shapes.

CLAGGUM

        2 teacups black treacle
        1 teacup cold water

Put the treacle and water into a heavy pan. Let it warm slowly,
then boil quickly to 237°F/114°C (soft ball). Pour into a greased
tin. When it is cold enough, flour the hands and make the toffee
into a lump. Pull it out until it becomes pale cream in colour and
twist into long sticks. This sweet was also called 'teasing candy'
and was very popular in Scotland around New Year.

LEMON BARLEY SUGAR

        1 lb cube sugar
        ¼ pint water
        1 dessertspoon lemon juice
        ½ teaspoon yellow food colouring
        Thinly peeled rind of 1 lemon

Put all the ingredients into a thick saucepan and stir over low heat until the sugar has dissolved. Bring to the boil and boil for 5 minutes. Take out the lemon rind. Boil to 280°F/140°C (soft crack). Take off the heat and allow to cool for 5 minutes. Pour into a shallow oiled tin and divide the mixture into thin strips. Twist and leave to set.

SUGAR MICE

    2 lb granulated sugar
    ¾ pint water
    3 oz powdered glucose
    Few drops of cochineal

Put the sugar and water into a heavy saucepan and heat gently until the sugar has dissolved. Add the glucose and boil to 237°F/114°C (soft ball). Cool without stirring until the mixture thickens. Pour on to a wet slab and work in the cochineal with a spatula until the mixture is firm and opaque and the colour is even. Form into 16 mice, moulding the ears carefully. Mark the eyes with a matchstick, or insert silver cake balls. Cut some clean white string into 3 in. lengths and press into the mice for tails. Leave to dry. Some mice can be left uncoloured.

EDINBURGH ROCK

    1 lb granulated sugar
    ½ pint water
    ¼ teaspoon cream of tartar
    Colouring and flavouring

Dissolve the sugar in the water over gentle heat. Add the cream of tartar and boil to 247°F/119°C (hard ball). Pour on to a marble slab and leave to cool for a few minutes. Turn sides to middle with a greased palette knife very gently. Repeat this process a few times as the mixture cools. Divide into portions and pour on a few drops of colouring and flavouring. Dust the hands with icing sugar and pull each piece lightly but firmly until dull and opaque. If the mixture gets very hard, warm it slightly as you pull it, but do not twist. Pull for 10-15 minutes until opaque and nearly set. Pull into strips, cut into even lengths about 3 in. long, and put on to waxed paper. Leave in a warm place for about 24 hours until powdery and soft. Store in a box lined with waxed paper. Be sure to match the colourings to the flavourings:

Pink: raspberry, strawberry, rose
Yellow: lemon, pineapple
Green: peppermint, almond
Brown: ginger, cinnamon, rum
Orange: orange
Mauve: violet

CARAWAY COMFITS
    1 lb cube sugar
    4 fl oz water
    8 oz caraway seeds
    Few drops of cochineal

Dissolve the sugar in the water and boil to a medium syrup. Drop in the caraway seeds, then remove them and put them into a sieve with a little flour. Shake well and leave to dry. Repeat the process several times until the sugar-coated seeds are the required size. Some of the comfits can be tinted pink during the final boiling with a little cochineal.

POPCORN
    2 oz dry sweetcorn kernels
    1 oz (approx.) vegetable oil or lard

This amount of corn kernels will make 3 pints of popcorn. Use a 3- or 4-pint saucepan with a lid and put it over a high heat.

Put the oil, using just enough to coat the bottom of the pan, and the sweetcorn kernels in together and cover with the lid. When popping starts in a minute or two, do not remove the lid, but shake the saucepan backwards and forwards over the heat until the popping noise stops. Take off the heat at once.

To make sweet popcorn, add 1 tablespoon granulated sugar with the corn.

TOFFEE POPCORN

> 2 oz butter
> 4 oz granulated sugar
> 4 oz golden syrup
> 1 dessertspoon malt vinegar
> Ready-made popcorn, as recipe above.

Melt the butter and add the sugar, stirring well. Pour in the syrup slowly and add the vinegar. Stir and bring to the boil. Cook to 247°F/119°C (hard ball), pour the toffee over the popcorn and mix well.

For *Chocolate Popcorn* add 1 tablespoon cocoa to the toffee mixture.

POPCORN BALLS

> 1 lb granulated sugar
> ¼ pint water
> 1 teaspoon lemon juice
> Ready-made popcorn, as recipe opposite

Heat together the sugar and water gently until dissolved. Bring to the boil and boil to 237°F/114°C (soft ball). Take off the heat and stir in the lemon juice. Pour over the popcorn and mix well. Dust hands with a little icing sugar, and as soon as the mixture is cool enough to handle, form into balls. Put on a wire cake rack to dry and wrap in waxed paper.

CINNAMON DROPS
   1 lb granulated sugar
   1 oz ground cinnamon
   ½ pint water
   2 egg whites, whisked

Mix the sugar and cinnamon thoroughly. Add the water and the whisked egg whites and mix very well. Put some clean white paper on to a baking tin. Drop the mixture in small spoonfuls on to the paper and dry at 250°F/120°C (Gas Mark ½) for 3 hours.

14 Presentation and Packaging

It is very important to pack sweets for presents or for sale neatly and attractively. As well as making the sweets look appetising, good packaging prevents damage to the sweets, so they won't get rubbed or crushed and decorations will remain intact.

USED PACKAGING
New boxes, bags and trimmings can be bought, but many items of used packaging can be saved for future use. If a sweetmaking session is planned for a bazaar or for present-giving, save up pretty boxes and tins from sweets or biscuits and some groceries. Save coloured paper, foil wrappings, paper shavings, ribbons and cords. Avoid using boxes which have contained soap or other scented, inedible goods.

SUGGESTED PACKAGING

1. Coffee tins with plastic lids make good containers for boiled sweets and toffees. Cover the tins with adhesive printed plastic, or paint them neatly, or use scraps of wallpaper. Cover the centre of the lid to match.
2. Foil containers, of the type used for baking and for freezing, make useful sweet containers. To seal, cover with a polythene bag, cling film or cellophane, drawn tautly over the surface of the sweets.
3. Glass jars with screw-tops or glass stoppers are always useful for packaging. The tops of coffee jars can be covered with a small piece of adhesive printed plastic.
4. Small, pretty biscuit tins can be finished with a strip of adhesive tape and a pretty ribbon or cord.
5. Small polythene boxes, of the type used for packed meals or for food freezing, can be sealed with tape or tied with ribbon or cord.
6. Cardboard boxes can be saved from other sweets, or folding white boxes can be specially purchased.
7. Cellophane bags with flaps to be sealed with tape or metal staples are good for selling sweets on stalls. If creams or fondants are packed in them, put the sweets on a piece of card cut to fit the bag.
8. Paper sacks can be made of large circles of waxed paper inside circles of crêpe paper. Run a line of stitches in embroidery silk near the top, to provide a drawstring.
9. Gifts of sweets that do not have to be posted can be packed in pretty cups and saucers, glass goblets, butter dishes, preserve jars, children's toy trains, etc., and give a personal touch to small presents.

HOW TO PACK

1. Wrap toffees and boiled sweets in foil or waxed paper. Tuck in the ends of the wrappers of neat square-shaped sweets,

like caramels; finish boiled sweets, humbugs, etc., with twisted ends.

2. Put truffles, creams, jellies, etc. into small, paper sweet cases. White cases look more professional than coloured ones, but dark brown ones are traditionally used for chocolates and truffles.

3. If possible, put some paper shavings in the bottom of boxes of tins to prevent movement, before packing sweets.

4. Arrange sweets with an eye to attractive colour blendings, and put a particularly attractive sweet in the centre of the box as an eye-catcher.

5. Separate rows of sweets with double paper strips, using greaseproof or waxed paper. Dark paper should be used for chocolates as they quickly mark white dividers. Thin card or foil can also be used as dividers.

6. Fill any spaces between sweets with crumpled soft paper so that the box will not rattle when filled.

7. Put a layer of card or paper between layers.

8. Cover the top layer with cling film or cellophane and top with a piece of padding (this can be bought by the yard, or saved from other boxes).

9. Cover with a lid and finish with cord, ribbons or ribbon rosettes.

10. Pack boxes for posting in corrugated card and strong brown paper.

PACKAGING SUPPLIERS
A wide range of foil, boxes, ribbons, etc., can be bought from stationers and chain stores.

Metric Conversion

In the kitchen, the new unit to replace the ounce is 25 g, and the one to replace the fluid ounce is 25 ml. This avoids awkward conversions and gives a satisfactory balance of liquids and solids in a recipe. A half ounce on this scale would be 12½ g, but is now usually quoted as 10 g or 15 g, depending on the results which are required. A 5 ml spoon can be used for small quantities.

WEIGHT TABLE

½ oz — 10 g or 15 g depending on results
1 oz — 25 g
2 oz — 50 g
3 oz — 75 g
4 oz — 100 g
8 oz — 200 g
1 lb — 400 g (meat and vegetable purchases are more likely to be 500 g or 0.5 kg)
2 lb — 800 g or 1 kg (meat and vegetable purchases are more likely to be 1000 g or 1 kg)

LIQUID TABLE

1 fl oz	—	25 ml
2 fl oz	—	50 ml
5 fl oz (¼ pint)	—	125 ml
½ pint	—	250 ml
¾ pint	—	375 ml
1 pint	—	500 ml
2 pint	—	1000 ml (1 litre)

Index